The Emotional Architect

Engineering The Human Variable For Technical Excellence

Lisa Akers

*For my Mom and Dad, who gave me the
foundation to build everything else.*

*For Leo and Mitch, who taught me what
unconditional support actually looks like—
and who have been my greatest teachers
in every system that matters.*

*For my beta readers—Justin Kratz, Chelsea
Partridge, Elyse Prescott, and Rachel Welch—
whose honest insights made this book immeasurably
better than I could have made it alone.*

*For Wendy Spurlin, my editor, who took a
manuscript and made it into a book—and
in doing so, created a physical manifestation
of the philosophy of a lifetime.*

Contents

This Isn't That Kind of Leadership Book

Prologue

I F YOU PICKED up this book hoping for tips on managing metrics and optimizing processes, put it back. This book is about something much harder: *leading humans who happen to do technical work.*

If you're the person everyone turns to when technical problems get messy—when stakeholders are fighting, when teams are stuck, when someone needs to translate between engineering brilliance and business reality—then keep reading. This book is for you.

You're the one who stays late when the code is broken, *and* because the team dynamics are broken. You're the one who gets pulled into meetings for your technical expertise, and because you can navigate the human complexity that surrounds technical decisions. You manage the systems and schedules, and also *emotions* and *egos* and organizational *politics.*

If you're exhausted from carrying emotional labor that should be shared across your team, this book might save your career or, more importantly, your life.

Before we go further, let me tell you something that shaped how I think about leadership. I majored in English in college—not exactly the typical path to technical leadership. One of the most valuable things about studying literature is that I read countless stories and analyzed character development across many different scenarios. I watched characters decide under pressure, saw what works and what destroys relationships, and observed leadership from hundreds of different perspectives.[1]

This was invaluable preparation for leadership. I gained the benefit of learning from fictional leaders, both brilliant and catastrophic, without having to make every mistake firsthand to understand the consequences. Through literature, I learned about human nature, motivation, conflict resolution, and the subtle dynamics that either build or break teams.

In literature, every great story hinges on how people react under extreme pressure. Years later, I would draw on those exact lessons in the most extreme environment imaginable. Spacecrafts aren't built by equations alone; they are built by humans—humans who get tired, get overwhelmed, and sometimes disagree on how to solve an impossible problem. The math is fixed, but the people are profoundly unpredictable.

I spent years preparing for a specific kind of pressure, but nothing quite prepares you for the moment you are named a Chief Engineer for the Artemis II mission.

In the world of human spaceflight, we don't just talk about "technical excellence" as a corporate value; it is a survival

---

1   This is sometimes called pattern recognition and reference sets. The context you gain from exploring dissimilar topics can illuminate unexpected paths and connections in the current situation. While commonly used in the context of artificial intelligence, the same principle applies to leadership. When drawing from philosophy, literature, psychology, organizational development, art, and parenting, a skilled leader sees options that aren't obvious from technical training and leadership texts.

requirement. When you are building the systems that will carry four human beings around the Moon for the first time in over half a century, the math has to be perfect. The physics are non-negotiable. As I sat in the high-stakes design reviews for the Orion spacecraft, it wasn't the math keeping me up at night.

The rockets were behaving. It was the human systems that were volatile. Artemis II is a "Human-in-the-Loop" mission. It's designed to test how the crew interacts with the technology in deep space. As Chief Engineer, my job was essentially the same thing on the ground: I was the human in the loop of a massive technical organization. I was responsible for the life support systems and the heat shield, sure—but my real work was tending the emotional infrastructure of the thousands of people building them.

I saw brilliant engineers paralyze themselves with the fear of being the one who missed a single decimal point that could cost a life. I saw stakeholders bartering over "acceptable risk" in ways that felt more like a poker game than a science project. Standing in the shadow of the world's most powerful rocket, the truth became unavoidable. Technical leadership is 10% engineering and 90% building the courage and honesty required for that engineering to matter. If the human architecture fails, the rocket doesn't even make it to the pad.

What I'm sharing in this book is my real-world experience—my successes, my mistakes, and the lessons learned through years of technical leadership. I hope that you'll be able to incorporate these insights without having to invest the time and emotional energy to live through every scenario yourself. What has worked for me may not be the perfect answer for your situation. Trust your inner wisdom. Take what resonates and leave what doesn't.

Who This Book Is For

This book is for technical leaders who have these traits:

Deep care for both technical excellence and the people who create it. Optimizing purely for the math feels impossible when the human cost is visible. The team dynamics are as important as delivery dates on the list of things that keep them awake at night. While others dismiss *human skills* as optional, they've learned that ignoring human systems makes technical systems fail.

Unrelenting work ethic. They're managing interpersonal conflicts that block technical progress, translating between teams that won't communicate, and carrying the emotional weight of decisions that affect both systems and people. They do their technical job plus everyone else's emotional labor, wondering why complex human dynamics always land on their desk.

Frustration with environments where empathy is optional. They are surrounded by people who dismiss *human skills* as nice-to-have, see emotional intelligence as weakness, and assume talented engineers should work like machines. Meanwhile, they watch projects fail because nobody wanted to address the organizational dysfunction that made technical work impossible.

Desire to lead differently. They're not interested in becoming the kind of manager who treats people like resources to be maximized. They want to create conditions where technical excellence and human flourishing happen together, but they've never seen a roadmap for building that kind of leadership capability while maintaining technical credibility.

Recognition that traditional leadership skills and advice don't work in technical environments. Generic management books promote *better communication* without recognizing that technical discussions require different skills than business presentations.

Who This Book Is NOT For

Let's be clear about who this book won't serve:

- Managers who believe technical employees should "leave emotions at the door"
- Professionals who define leadership through processes, metrics, and authority structures
- Teams searching for quick fixes, simple frameworks, or five-step solutions to complex human problems

The work described here takes time and a willingness to examine patterns and assumptions. Anyone not ready to acknowledge they might be part of the problem they're trying to solve should put this book down and come back later.

Why This Matters Now

The technical world has reached a breaking point that makes this kind of leadership essential, not optional. We're living through the most complex engineering challenges in human history. We have space programs with decade-long timelines and billion-dollar consequences. Engineers are building software systems that touch millions of lives daily. There are thousands of infrastructure projects that must work perfectly on the first try. Technical complexity keeps growing, and the human cost of failure has grown even faster.

When systems fail now, they break spectacularly and publicly. Technical teams that can't read team dynamics miss the early warning signs. Organizations that can't build psychological safety lose critical information when people are afraid to speak up. Environments that burn out their best people create the very crises they're trying to prevent.

Meanwhile, the talent pool is transforming. Engineers entering the workforce today expect psychological safety, clear communication, and leaders who see them as whole humans, not a box full of technical resources. They'll leave organizations that treat empathy as a weakness. They're choosing companies based on culture, not technical challenges alone.

Organizations that figure this out first will have an enormous competitive advantage. They'll catch problems earlier, innovate faster, and retain the talent that everyone else is fighting over. They'll build the kind of technical teams that can handle the impossible challenges ahead.

Companies that don't will keep cycling through technical talent, managing crisis after crisis, wondering why their best people keep leaving for competitors who get it.

Instead of making engineering softer, successful leaders are making it more effective. The future belongs to technical leaders who understand that in our interconnected, high-stakes world, the ultimate technical skill is the ability to engineer human systems that enable technical excellence. Emotional architecture matters for technical teams—can you become proficient at it before your competitors do?

What You'll Learn

Forget perfect leadership. That myth leads straight to burnout. This book will teach you to be an Emotional Architect: someone who designs the human systems that allow technical brilliance to work.

Move from Firefighting to Blueprinting: Most leaders spend their day reacting to "technical" emergencies that are actually human system failures in disguise. You'll learn to spot the cracks in team trust or the *invisible transactions* that lead to missed deadlines before they turn into a crisis that requires a hero.

Develop X-Ray Vision for Technical Failures: When a project stalls, is it a bad requirements document, or is it a psychological safety problem? We'll look at how to decode the human dynamics hiding inside your Jira tickets and design reviews.

Master Conversations That Actually Resolve Things: We've all been in meetings where everyone talks but nothing changes. You'll gain frameworks for handling emotional laziness and conflict in a way that makes people feel safe enough to bring you their real concerns instead of sanitized status reports.

Multiply Your Impact by Letting Go: If you are the only person who can solve a specific problem, you are the bottleneck. You'll learn how to mentor your team so they make the same high-quality decisions you would, allowing your influence to grow even as your direct involvement decreases.

Stop the "Emotional Labor Dump": You'll learn how to stop being the designated repository for everyone else's anxiety and risk. We will design a system where labor is shared appropriately across the team, making your career sustainable for decades rather than just until the next milestone.

A Warning About the Work Ahead

This book will ask you to question everything you think you know about technical leadership. Some of it will be uncomfortable.

Your technical expertise may be your biggest liability. The same drive for perfection that made you a brilliant engineer can turn you into a micromanaging impediment as a leader. If you are always the person with the answers, you aren't being help-ful—you're training your team to stop thinking.

We often mistake conflict avoidance for kindness. It isn't. When you refuse to address a performance issue or a boundary violation, you aren't being "nice"—you're being cowardly. Those problems don't disappear; they metastasize.

You may also discover that your burnout is self-inflicted. We often unconsciously volunteer for everyone else's emotional labor because being the "fixer" makes us feel valuable, even as it destroys our well-being.

Realize that becoming a better leader will likely disappoint people who benefit from the current dysfunction. Some team members want you to solve their problems; some managers want you to carry their risks. When you finally start building systems instead of being the hero, not everyone will thank you.

If you aren't ready to look honestly at your own patterns, put this book down. But if your current way of leading leaves you exhausted, keep reading. The discomfort you feel isn't a sign that you're doing something wrong—it's a sign that you're finally doing the work that matters.

How to Use This Book

This book tells the story of how technical experts become technical leaders. It follows a logical progression from an individual contributor mindset to sustainable leadership capability. To get the most out of your growth journey, follow these guidelines:

Begin with Chapter 1 and read sequentially. Each chapter builds on the previous ones, with frameworks and concepts interconnecting throughout.

The personal application sections deserve attention. The "How This Shows Up Everywhere" sections in each chapter aren't filler. They recognize that the same skills that make technical leaders effective will improve every relationship in life.

Implementation works best incrementally. Pick one concept from each chapter and practice until it becomes natural before moving to the next. Skill development is iterative, not linear. Working through this book may take time. That deliberate, intentional pace serves the journey well.

Leadership is learned in community, not in isolation. Find peers, mentors, or coaching relationships where discussing and practicing these concepts becomes possible.

Keep the Playbook sections handy for reference. After finishing the book, the Playbook sections in each chapter become helpful guides for specific challenges, whether professional or personal. Regular referencing of these skills reinforces the learning.

Timeline

The chapters in this book are organized by complexity rather than in chronological order. Real leadership development isn't linear. I learned these lessons through overlapping experiences, repeated mistakes, and gradual insights that built on each other over more than three decades in aerospace engineering.

You'll find references to early career experiences alongside recent challenges because that's how growth happens. We revisit the same fundamental challenges at deeper levels as our responsibilities expand. The skills for reading a room that I needed as a project lead became more nuanced when applied to senior stakeholder conflicts. The trust-building approaches that worked with a small team required adaptation for cross-organizational relationships.

My goal here is to show you how these emotional architecture skills develop and compound over time, through different roles, different challenges, and different organizational contexts.

The Promise

Commitment to this work—genuine commitment, not passive reading—transforms technical leaders into the people others study to understand how they achieve extraordinary results from ordinary teams.

When you stop being the hero who saves every project, you become the architect who designs conditions where the projects save themselves. Problems are caught early not because you found them, but because the system did.

This shift transforms your role from the person everyone depends on into a mentor who intentionally builds independence. Your team makes the decisions you would have made, handles the conflicts you would have mediated, and solves the problems you would have solved. Your influence multiplies exponentially because you've stopped creating followers and started developing leaders.

Team members make the same decisions their leader would have made, handle conflicts their leader would have mediated, and solve problems their leader would have solved. Influence multiplies exponentially because the focus shifts from creating followers to developing leaders.

Technical excellence and human flourishing aren't competing priorities; they are a feedback loop. Teams deliver better code and more resilient hardware precisely because they feel safe enough to share a 'half-baked' idea or challenge a senior's assumption. Innovation should be a byproduct of a team that trusts each other, not a 2:00 AM act of heroism fueled by caffeine and the fear of missing a deadline.

You'll develop a different kind of confidence. Those difficult conversations that used to cause sleepless nights? You'll see them as technical diagnostics—valuable information about a flaw in the human system. Organizational politics stop being a drain on your energy and start being just another variable to work with and around without losing your integrity.

Your career sustains and energizes across decades, not just until the next burnout. You'll learn to recognize patterns before they become problems, set boundaries that protect capacity, and maintain effectiveness without sacrificing well-being.

You'll experience the profound satisfaction that comes from building a legacy by enabling others to exceed their own expectations. The best leaders aren't remembered for personal technical achievements. They're remembered for the people they mentored, the teams they built, and the culture they created that continued improving long after they moved on. The gap between individual excellence and leadership effectiveness is where all the real growth happens.

The Human Variable

Throughout this book, we'll explore what I call the "human variable." I define this as the complex emotional and interpersonal dynamics that either enable or constrain technical excellence. Being fluent in this framework means recognizing that in any technical system, the most unpredictable and influential component is often the humans operating within it.

Think of it this way: you wouldn't design a spacecraft without accounting for thermal expansion, vibration, and radiation effects. Yet most people try to build teams without considering the invisible human forces that determine whether brilliant people can work together effectively: how trust develops, how people communicate under pressure, whether teams feel safe enough to surface problems early.

Technical leaders who ignore the human variable do so at their own peril. The most elegant technical solution fails if the people implementing it are demoralized or working against each other. The most efficient process falls apart if team members don't trust each other enough to communicate problems early. The most brilliant technical insight never emerges if the person who has it doesn't feel safe to share their half-formed idea. The human variable is what determines whether technical excellence is possible.

This book teaches you to design for the human variable the same way you'd design for any other critical system component—with the same precision and the same respect for its complexity. You'll learn to engineer conditions that bring out people's best technical thinking instead of hoping good results will emerge from poorly designed human systems.

Important boundary: This work is about creating conditions where healthy, functional people can do their best technical work.

You won't become a therapist, counselor, or personal development coach for your team members. If you consistently manage someone's personal crises, provide ongoing emotional support for non-work issues, or try to fix deep-seated behavioral patterns, you've moved beyond leadership into territory that requires professional expertise you likely don't possess.

When these situations arise, and they will, your role is to connect people with appropriate resources (Employee Assistance Programs, Human Resources support, professional counseling) while maintaining clear boundaries about what support you can and cannot provide as a technical leader. Leadership is about creating systems and conditions that bring out people's existing capabilities. Therapy is about helping people develop new capabilities or heal from past trauma. These are different skills with different boundaries, and confusing them serves no one well.

Ready?

The technical world needs more visionaries who understand that the most complex systems aren't machines—they're the human beings who design, build, and operate those machines. If you're ready to engineer human systems with the same rigor applied to technical systems, let's begin.

A Note on the Stories: The examples in this book are inspired by real experiences, though I've changed names and details to protect privacy and security. Some stories are composites of a collection of experiences. Good engineers know every answer includes "it depends." Take what serves your situation and adapt the rest. You know your context best. My goal is simply to show you what's possible when technical leadership includes intentional emotional architecture.

An Email and an Opportunity

Chapter 1

THE EMAIL WAS short. Too short.

"Lisa, I've decided to pursue other opportunities. My last day will be Friday."

I stared at the screen. Something between panic and rage built in my chest. Four months into the most challenging project of my career, my co-engineer—the one person who understood both the technical complexity and the customer relationships we'd spent months building—was walking away.

Just like that. No transition plan. No knowledge transfer. No, *let me help you figure this out*. Just… gone.

I looked through my office window at the team scattered across the high bay floor. The team that everyone else had quietly written off. The ones who weren't part of the "in-crowd." The technicians who were skilled but somehow always got the leftover assignments while the high-profile work went to others.

My team now. All mine.

The Path That Led Here

Sitting in that office, processing the shock of what lay ahead, I couldn't help but think about the journey that brought me to this moment. Nothing in my career prepared me for what I was about to face.

I've wanted to work in the space industry since I was very young, watching those grainy Apollo landing videos and dreaming of becoming an astronaut. My dream shaped every decision I made: attending the US Air Force Academy, pursuing engineering, building my entire identity around the technical excellence that would someday take me to space.

The dream took a sharp detour during my graduation physical when I learned I was both too short and far too nearsighted to qualify for astronaut training. Something else was born during those four years at the Academy—an understanding of what leadership meant. There's a certain gravitas that comes from being a young military officer who may at some point be asked to lead people into an operation that might mean their death. That reality grounded me in figuring out the great responsibility of being a leader.

I was fortunate to work in space operations in the Air Force, including a brief assignment at the Space Environment Forecast Center. After the military, I joined Lockheed Martin as a test engineer for West Coast launch operations, leading cross-functional teams to assemble and launch rockets. That role taught me about leading people who don't do the same work as you do. I was leading engineers, quality inspectors, technicians, and managers who all needed to stay engaged on particular tasks while navigating multiple stakeholders like contracts managers, safety personnel, and schedulers.

Then I moved to the commercial satellite communications industry, dealing with international customers, technical challenges, and complex interpersonal dynamics. This job gave me extensive experience talking with people from varied backgrounds who had different goals and engaged in discussions very differently. I learned about collaboration and the nuances of listening to what is said, and more importantly, what is *not* said.

After taking about five years off to be home with my young children, I returned to the space world on the Orion human spaceflight program, where I've been evolving and expanding my skills for the last 19 years. I joined the Chief Engineer's office in 2020 and made it my mission to build up the next generation of technical leaders through my Technical Leadership Pipeline, talks around the country, my weekly email messages, and this book.

I'd been a successful individual contributor, a capable project lead, someone who could offer technical advice and watch teams implement solutions. I was good at being an expert consultant, but here I was having to lead people through uncertainty when I didn't have the answers myself.

The Technical Leader I Thought I Was

Until the moment my co-worker resigned, I'd defined myself by my technical capabilities. I was the engineer who could dive deep into complex problems and emerge with elegant solutions. I was the one who stayed late to perfect the analysis, who caught the errors others missed, who could explain complicated systems to anyone who asked.

I thought that's what leadership was: being the smartest person in the room, having the right answers, solving the problems that stumped everyone else. That email from my departing colleague shattered my illusion completely. Suddenly, the biggest problem in front of me wasn't technical at all. It was human.

I had a team that was labeled as difficult, lacking ambition, and hard to work with. My impossible deadline was eight months away. Here I had no idea how to lead people who didn't believe

in themselves. The engineering part felt manageable (sort of).
The human part felt terrifying.

The First Truth

When you step into technical leadership, no one tells you most
of your problems won't be technical ones. They'll be people problems wearing technical clothes.

- That failed component probably happened because someone felt rushed and didn't speak up about a concern they'd
  noticed.
- That schedule delay likely started when two teams made
  different assumptions about interfaces, and no one created
  space for those assumptions to surface.
- That budget overrun often traces back to someone
  being afraid to deliver bad news early, so small problems
  compounded into expensive ones.

Standing in my office, watching the team through the window,
I realized I was looking at an emotional architecture problem
(but I didn't know that at the time).

Eric believed he could build anything—but only if he felt
safe to think through problems without someone demanding
immediate answers.

Maria had incredible attention to detail—but she'd been
burned before by managers who dismissed her observations as
"overthinking."

Tom could see problems coming—but he'd learned to stay
quiet because previous supervisors labeled his caution as a "negative attitude."

Sarah asked the hard questions—but she'd been told too
many times that she was being *difficult*.

They weren't broken. They were protecting themselves. Instead of trying to make it my job to fix them, I needed to create conditions where they could show up as their most capable selves.

A Weekend of Uncertainty

That Friday night, after receiving my colleague's resignation email, I sat in my empty office longer than I should have. The high bay was quiet. The team had left for the day, and I was staring at an impossible project. I'd spent my entire career being the technical expert who brought answers. Now I was facing a challenge that couldn't be solved with better engineering or more hours. I needed something from my team that I didn't know how to ask for.

I thought about calling my mentor, but what would I say? "Help, my team doesn't trust me, and I don't know how to fix it?" I was not ready to admit I wasn't ready for leadership. Maybe that was true, but it wasn't helpful.

Instead, I thought about the teams I'd been part of that were successful. Not just the ones that delivered results, but the ones where I was excited to show up, where problems were like interesting puzzles instead of threats, where everyone seemed to bring their best thinking. Those teams had something my current team didn't: psychological safety. Not the touchy-feely kind, but the practical kind where people could say, *I don't know, I'm worried about this, or What if we tried something different?* without fear of judgment.

As I sat thinking over the weekend, I realized I'd been trying to earn their respect through technical competence. I'd been leading as if people were technical resources to be optimized. This wasn't a technical problem. This was a human systems problem. Human systems require different tools. These were humans who needed to understand why their work mattered, feel safe to voice concerns, and believe their expertise was valued. What I really needed was their trust. Trust isn't built through expertise. It's built through connection.

On Sunday evening, the idea for a simple conversation over coffee came to me. It felt too cheesy to even try, and I almost talked myself out of it three times before Monday morning. Could it be as simple as just asking these people how we can work together to solve this challenge? I was afraid of admitting that I didn't have the answers. I was worried about how they would perceive me if I asked them for help. I didn't want to shift my focus from technical solutions, but I had no idea how to lead us through the next few months.

Coffee and Connections

Walking into that break room Monday morning, I had no idea if this would work. I just knew what I'd been doing wasn't working, and I was finally ready to try something different. I did something I'd never done before as a leader. Instead of diving straight into technical discussions and the day's agenda, I invited everyone to meet in the break room.

"Bring your coffee," I said. "Let's just… talk."

They looked at me as if I had three heads. Engineers don't do feelings, right? We do facts and data and problem-solving.

I had spent the weekend realizing I was out of my depth. I needed the team to do more than just execute; I needed them to be brave. Brave enough to tell me I was wrong, to share the stupid ideas that actually solve problems, and to stick with me when the comfort zone was a mile back in the rearview mirror. I didn't recognize it as a *need* then—I just felt the weight of not having the answer and the quiet hope that we could find one together.

This conversation needed to be more than building relationships. I was laying the emotional foundation that would allow technical excellence to emerge. Trust isn't built through technical competence alone. It requires intentionally designing connections that enable vulnerability and curiosity.

The first coffee conversation was awkward. I asked how everyone was doing and got the standard "fine" responses. Eric stared into his coffee. Maria checked her watch. I almost gave up and went back to discussing work.

When Sarah mentioned she'd been volunteering with a turtle rescue program, *something shifted.* Eric showed genuine curiosity about how turtle rehabilitation worked. Maria shared that her daughter was starting high school and was nervous about the transition. Tom talked about coaching his son's soccer team: how different it was working with kids versus adults.

Nothing earth-shattering. Just human connection.

I'd love to say our team dynamic shifted right away. This took time. Gradually, over the next several weeks, I watched these "difficult" people transform into the most collaborative team I'd ever worked with.

As our team's confidence grew and our results improved, I noticed patterns I'd previously missed. I saw subtle dynamics in meetings, unspoken tensions between stakeholders, the way technical discussions could go sideways for reasons that had nothing to do with engineering.

I was seeing what I'd been blind to all along: every technical conversation happens within a human context. If you can't read that context, you can't lead effectively, no matter how brilliant your technical solutions might be.

The Players in This Story

Let me introduce you to the team members you'll encounter throughout this book. Over the coming chapters, you'll see how each of them navigates different leadership challenges, and you'll meet other characters who add depth to these lessons. I've changed names and details throughout this book, so if you encounter anyone who sounds familiar, it's definitely a coincidence.

Eric is a methodical problem-solver who needs space to think without pressure for immediate answers. You'll see him again when we explore how smart people can disagree productively.

Maria is a detail-oriented technician whose observations were dismissed as "overthinking." Her story continues in the chapter on building trust foundations.

Tom is a cautious technician who'd learned to stay quiet about potential problems. His experience becomes central to our discussion of emotional labor and speaking up.

Sarah is the question-asker who'd been labeled "difficult" for challenging assumptions. Her journey illustrates the art of technical compromise.

Tyler is an emerging leader who becomes central to our exploration of leadership development. Tyler's story shows what happens when someone is ready to grow and how the multiplication effect of good mentoring can transform entire organizations.

You'll also meet **Beck**, a manager facing impossible organizational pressures, and others whose experiences shaped how I understand what it means to lead technical teams through human challenges.

Each of these people gave depth to the way I define emotional architecture. I learned pieces of the structure from each of them. Seeing them interact with each other and with me helped me define key pieces of the framework I'll share in this book.

The Emotional Architect Awakening

Without having words for it yet, I was becoming an Emotional Architect. Although it would take years to form in my mind, this launch vehicle build and test meant more for me and this team than building a test vehicle. The work I was doing built the *emotional infrastructure* that would allow technical excellence to emerge. Every conversation was a design choice. Every interaction was structural engineering. Every decision about how we worked together laid the foundation for what we could accomplish.

When I asked Eric to share his technical insights instead of telling him what I needed, he offered creative solutions I never would have found on my own. With him, I built an emotional environment where his technical insights could emerge. By designing our interactions to prioritize his thinking over my immediate question, I created space for the kind of innovation that happens when people feel genuinely heard. In one case, he recommended using a tool designed for a different purpose that worked well for our unusual assembly process.

When I asked Maria to help me write procedures that captured not only what to do but why it mattered, our error rate plummeted. She knew it was important to capture the details about why we do the work in a certain way so that when things weren't quite perfect, the team could make smart choices about how to proceed.

When I created space for Tom to voice concerns without being labeled negative, he caught problems before they became expensive failures. When people feel seen and heard without feeling dismissed, they're more willing to be open with their ideas.

When I encouraged Sarah's hard questions instead of shutting them down, she helped us avoid three potential design pitfalls. These were easy to miss—the design was mature and I knew it like the back of my own hand. As a newcomer, she pointed out details I took for granted.

This felt strange and empowering. I wasn't managing them. I was building a team culture that accounted for the human variable.

The Transformation in Action: What Changed and How

The transition from protective habits to excellent collaboration was tangible. It appeared in specific, observable ways that took everyone, myself included, by surprise.

Eric's Evolution:

Before: I'd ask Eric for a timeline estimate; he'd give me a vague answer like "probably a couple of weeks" and then disappear into his work. If I pressed for specifics, he'd get defensive and say something like, "It'll take as long as it takes."

After: Eric broke down problems out loud. "This assembly has three main challenges," he'd say. "The first two I can solve this week, but the third one—I need to think about that. Can I get back to you on Friday with a real timeline?" He offered creative alternatives: "What if we approach this differently? I have an idea that might cut our time in half."

I saw the shift when Eric voluntarily stayed late to help Sarah understand a mechanical connection she struggled with. Earlier, he would have fixed it himself and moved on.

Maria's Transformation:

Before: Maria would catch errors in procedures but phrase her concerns tentatively, "Maybe this is wrong…" or "I might be overthinking this…" She'd document issues thoroughly but wouldn't push back when her recommendations were dismissed.

After: Maria presented her observations with confidence, "I found three issues in this procedure that could be challenges." She proposed solutions instead of identifying problems. "Here's what I think we should change and why."

I knew this was working when Maria interrupted a review meeting to point out a potential safety issue. Old Maria would have written it in an email afterward. The new Maria stopped the meeting and said, "We need to address this before we move forward."

Tom's Revolution:

Before: Tom learned to keep his concerns to himself. He'd see potential problems but wouldn't speak up because previous supervisors labeled him "negative" or told him he was "borrowing trouble."

After: Tom became our early warning system. "I'm worried about this timeline," he'd say. "Here's what I think could go wrong and what we could do to prevent it." He framed concerns in terms of mission success rather than being the one who always said "no."

His breakthrough came when he caught a potential issue that would have delayed our test by weeks. Instead of staying quiet, he presented a complete analysis: problem identification, impact assessment, and three potential solutions. Senior management went out of their way to thank him for the save.

Sarah's Breakthrough:

Before: Sarah asked excellent questions and learned to apologize for them. "I'm sorry for bringing this up…" Her probing questions came across as challenges to authority rather than genuine curiosity.

After: Sarah learned to frame her questions as mission-focused collaboration, "Help me understand why we chose this approach over alternative X," or "What would happen if we considered this constraint differently?"

Her transformation crystallized when she questioned a design assumption that we'd all accepted with little consideration. Instead of getting defensive, I said, "That's a really good point. Let's take a look." Her questions led us to a much better solution.

The Measurable Impact: These were more than feel-good changes. They showed up in our metrics:

- Error rates dropped by 40% because people felt safe pointing out problems.
- Timeline estimates became 90% more accurate because people could admit uncertainties.
- Problem-solving speed doubled because we were using everyone's expertise.
- Management's confidence in our team went from skeptical to positive.

The most important change was this: they solved problems without me. What began as a crisis of leadership became proof that emotional architecture creates technical excellence.

How This Shows Up Everywhere

The funny thing about emotional architecture is that once you build it consciously, you realize it's been the foundation of every relationship in your life.

Think about the people you turn to when you need support. Chances are, they're not the smartest people you know. They're the ones who create emotional safety, who listen without judging, who ask questions that help you think more clearly rather than questions that make you feel defensive.

The same principles that were transforming my technical team showed up in other relationships too. The patience I'd learned when Eric needed space to think made me a better parent when my kids were working through problems. The curiosity I'd developed about Maria's expertise improved every one of my relationships. This skill was essential to my personal and professional growth. It altered the way I presented myself in all areas. Like any architecture, you have to keep working on it. The day you stop is the day it starts crumbling. The skills that transform technical teams are the same ones that strengthen every relationship in your life when applied with wisdom.

The View from Outside:
The Friction of Change

While I was seeing internal transformation, my managers and leaders weren't so sure. During those early coffee chats, we were all clearly charting unfamiliar territory. There was a profound sense of uncertainty and concern vibrating through the hallways about whether we could meet the looming delivery dates or if the rocket would work like it was supposed to.

I was at a crossroads. I needed to offload some of my heavy technical responsibilities onto my team so I could actually lead, which meant I needed them to step up and take on more than they ever had. Internally, I was terrified. I was afraid they were not ready, and I was deeply concerned about whether I could give up control of the technical "truth" I had spent my career mastering.

Meanwhile, my management team was under fire. They were getting pressure every day from stakeholders to keep us on schedule. In that high-pressure environment, finding myself leading "solo"—focusing on the team's internal health rather than just the technical output—felt like a huge blow to our collective ability to keep performing. My decision to focus on my team and not spend as much time "managing up" added to the management team's discomfort. In hindsight, I could have done a better job keeping people in the loop to ease their worries, but at the time, I was too focused on the crisis in front of me to invest much effort up the chain. I was building a sanctuary for my team, but to those outside, it looked like I was building a wall.

When It Goes Wrong: My Leadership Learning Curve

This shift didn't happen overnight, and it certainly didn't happen without a few spectacular crashes. Years before I was named a Chief Engineer for Orion, I had to learn the hard way that technical expertise is not a substitute for leadership.

Back then, I'd been able to make do with my own technical skills. I could write the work instructions, offer the "correct" insights, and the team would implement the solution. I was an excellent individual contributor; I didn't have to lead. But as I moved into higher-stakes roles, the load became too heavy to carry alone.

I started looking for answers, reading Simon Sinek's *Start with Why*. His ideas resonated deeply with the sense of responsibility I'd practiced in the Air Force. I began talking about why our work mattered—shifting us out of the petty squabbles that derail teams under pressure. In my eagerness to apply these new insights, I made some pretty big mistakes. I fell into the trap of projecting potential onto people who weren't actually interested in the work of growth.

I worked with one individual who showed flashes of exceptional insight during high-stakes moments. I immediately saw the possibilities—imagining how they could grow into a fantastic technical leader. I made it my mission to create opportunities for them, advocating for their visibility and investing hours in their development. At first, it seemed to work; they rose to the occasion when the spotlight was on.

I mistakenly assumed their best performance was their typical ability. What I saw as untapped potential was their maximum output. It was a performance they could access when the stakes were high, but not something they could maintain consistently. They were interested in the outcome of growth (the title, the recognition) but not the process (the daily practice and uncomfortable self-reflection).

I didn't like the lesson that came from this. It still frustrates me to see that people will rise to the level of their actual capacity, not the level of your expectations for them. As an emotional architect, your greatest strength—seeing what people could be— can become your greatest blind spot when you mistake your vision of their potential for their genuine commitment to growth.

I also struggled with the boundary between supporting someone and carrying their emotional labor for them. One team member was technically gifted but consistently struggled with interpersonal conflicts. Instead of helping them develop conflict resolution skills, I constantly smoothed over their interactions and made excuses for them. I wasn't building their architecture; I was acting as a temporary prop. When they eventually moved to another team, they collapsed because I hadn't taught them how to stand on their own.

These were the scars I carried with me into the Artemis program. By the time I sat in the design reviews for the Orion spacecraft, I knew that emotional architecture wasn't about making everyone successful regardless of their investment. It was about creating the conditions where the people who were willing to do the work could finally flourish.

The Flight Test

Eight months later, in the pre-dawn hours of a summer Florida morning, we were standing on the deck of a ship off the coast of the launch pad, watching our test vehicle go through its final checks. The tension was palpable, as it is before any launch. Thoughts of the build process, all the ways we solved problems, fixed broken hardware, and accepted less-than-perfect conditions ran through my brain. When the booster ignited, I mentally counted the seconds until the next critical event. Each one happened on schedule and exactly as planned. The test was absolutely perfect. As we hugged and celebrated, we reflected on the team we had built. This kind of team experience is rare, and we all knew it. We overcame technical challenges, unexpected personal obstacles, and skepticism from our management team.

The same technicians who were labeled as "difficult" had accomplished something that made the senior management take notice.

They didn't just build a test vehicle. They'd built themselves into leaders. What I took from all of this is that technical leadership was about creating conditions where everyone else can be technically excellent.

The jackets I bought for them at the end (with our mission patches) were symbols of what happens when you invest in emotional architecture first and let technical brilliance follow. When I wear my jacket, it reminds me of how far we've come and inspires me to keep going.

Reflection Framework: Building Emotional Architecture in Your Leadership

Take a moment to consider your own relationship with creating conditions for your team's success. The goal isn't to judge yourself, but to honestly assess where you are so you can decide where you want to go.

Think About Your Current Team

When someone brings you a concern, do they come with just the problem, or do they also share their thinking about possible solutions? The latter suggests you've created conditions where people feel safe offering their judgment, not just escalating issues.

Do team members admit when they don't know something, or do they hedge and avoid uncertainty? The framework you've built shows up in people's willingness to be uncertain in front of you.

When was the last time you learned something personal about a team member that had nothing to do with work? Human connection is the foundation that allows emotional architecture to function—you can't design conditions for people you see only as technical resources.

If you removed yourself from the team tomorrow, would they continue functioning at the same level, or would everything grind to a halt? The answer reveals whether you've created capability or accidentally designed dependence.

One Thing to Try This Week

Create space for one genuine conversation with a team member about something other than deliverables. Ask about their weekend, their interests, and what they're learning. Notice your own discomfort with "unproductive" time and their response to your curiosity. This is emotional architecture in practice—recognizing that human connection enables the conditions where technical excellence can emerge.

Playbook:
Building Trust Through
Intentional Connection

Keep the Playbook sections handy for reference. After finishing the book, the Playbook sections in each chapter become helpful guides for specific challenges, whether professional or personal. Regularly referencing these skills reinforces the learning.

When Your Team Operates Like Disconnected Resources

If you realize you know your team members' technical skills but nothing about them as humans, you're missing the foundation for emotional architecture. Watch out for technically competent but emotionally disconnected teams, environments where personal sharing feels unprofessional, and your own discomfort with "non-productive" conversations.

Start with low-stakes opportunities. Say, "I'm grabbing coffee, anyone want to join?" or "Let's start our meeting with a quick check-in—how is everyone doing?" You're designing space for people to be human, not just functions.

Notice what happens when you share something personal. I spent the weekend hiking with my kids creates different conditions than I worked all weekend. Model the human connection that enables honest technical communication.

You're creating enough human connection that people feel safe being real with each other about technical challenges. Skip the forced bonding and artificial team-building exercises.

When Previous Systems Damaged the Foundation

If you inherit a team where previous leadership damaged the emotional architecture, or you've made mistakes that eroded the foundation, rebuilding requires consistency over time. Watch out for teams with protective behaviors, people who won't speak up even when they should, or your own impatience with the slow pace of rebuilding.

Acknowledge the reality without dwelling on it: "I know creating safe conditions takes time, especially if past experiences taught you to be cautious. I'm committed to building that foundation through my actions, not just my words."

Follow through relentlessly on small commitments. If you say you'll look into something, do it. If you promise confidentiality, maintain it absolutely. Emotional architecture rebuilds one kept promise at a time.

Create transparent decision-making processes. Explain your reasoning, especially when you make unpopular choices. Using the framework: "Here's what I'm considering, here's what I'm worried about, and here's why I'm choosing this path," builds structural integrity even when people disagree with your decision.

When You've Accidentally Designed Dependence

If you realize you're drawn to being the person everyone depends on, examine whether you've built capability or inadvertently created a system that requires you to do the work. Watch for team members who won't decide without you, your own satisfaction when people need you to solve their problems, or resentment that you're carrying everyone's weight.

Shift what you're designing for. Instead of conditions where "I solved another crisis," create conditions where "My team solved a crisis without me."

When someone asks for help, resist the urge to provide immediate answers. Ask, "What have you already tried?" and "What would you do if I weren't available?" Notice your discomfort with their struggle and observe their growth through working it out. You're creating conditions where your absence doesn't create chaos because you've built capability into the system rather than reinforcing dependence on you.

When Connection Feels Like Poor Engineering

If building human connections with your team feels awkward or unprofessional, you're not alone. Many technical leaders learned that emotional distance equals professionalism. Watch for your discomfort with conversations about non-work topics, concern that human connection undermines authority, or fear that caring about people makes you vulnerable.

Start where you're comfortable. If coffee chats feel too intimate, try "How was your weekend?" during a one-on-one. If that feels forced, share something about yourself first: "I tried a new restaurant this weekend and it was terrible" creates space for others to share without pressure.

Connection requires seeing people as humans, not just functions. Asking about someone's interests, remembering details they shared previously, and showing genuine curiosity are all part of designing the emotional infrastructure that enables technical work. Deep personal disclosure remains optional.

The most brilliant technical solution fails if the people implementing it don't feel safe enough to surface problems early. Human connection enables the conditions for technical excellence.

When Someone Needs Support Beyond Your Design Scope

If you realize a team member is bringing personal struggles that require professional support beyond your scope as a leader, maintain clear boundaries while still caring. Watch for ongoing emotional crises, requests for personal advice on non-work issues, or your own discomfort with becoming someone's therapist rather than their leader.

Respond with care and appropriate boundaries: "I can see this is really difficult for you. Our Employee Assistance Program offers confidential counseling that might be helpful. Let me know what support you need from me to navigate this at work."

You can care about people without carrying their personal struggles for them. Your role is to architect conditions where healthy, functional people can do their best technical work.

When someone needs therapeutic support, connecting them with appropriate resources is the most caring leadership action.

Leadership and therapy require different expertise. Confusing them serves no one well, regardless of how much you care about the person struggling.

The Journey Ahead

That flight test gave me a different context and perspective on technical work and how it fits into the larger theme of technical leadership. I realized that true technical leadership extends beyond technical skills into the complex realm of human dynamics. It requires just as much precision and practice as any technical discipline, but is instead focused on trust, clarity, psychological safety, and human motivation. My success with Eric, Maria, Tom, and Sarah proved that my ideas worked. It also revealed how much I still needed to learn.

I'd created that breakthrough largely through intuition and patient one-on-one conversations in a relatively controlled environment. My next challenge was to understand how to apply these principles in complex situations when multiple organizations were involved, when the stakes were higher, or when cultural differences and hidden pressures shaped every interaction.

I thought I could simply apply the same approach to any technical conversation, only to discover that I missed half the information I needed to be effective. Before you can build emotional architecture, you must see the invisible systems that will either support or undermine your efforts. You have to learn to read the room.

In the years since, I've refined what I learned in that high bay into frameworks and practices that work across industries, team sizes, and technical challenges. It all started with understanding that every technical conversation happens within a human context. The skills you'll develop throughout this book aren't just about becoming a better leader today; they're about building a leadership legacy that multiplies your impact across time and organizations.

Reading the Room: When Technical Expertise Isn't Enough

Chapter 2

OUR FLIGHT TEST was in July 2019. After we finished up the post-flight test review, the facility refurbishment, and the paperwork closure, I moved back into my office in Denver and accepted a role in the chief engineering office.

Settling back into a climate-controlled office after the adrenaline of a launch pad is always a jarring adjustment. In the field, the mission is the only thing that matters; in the Chief Engineering Office, the mission is often buried under the relentless hum of coordination and consensus-building. I was riding the high of a successful test, feeling more confident than ever in my technical authority. I assumed that because I had the data and the title, the human side of the job would simply fall into place. I was wrong.

As is typical of most days, my calendar was full of back-to-back meetings. One call with a supplier, scheduled right before lunch, didn't seem like it would be any different from the dozen others I'd had that week. I'd prepared for it the way I'd prepared for everything else that summer: with cold, hard facts.

The call started exactly as planned, with two engineering teams discussing the electrical interface between our flight computer and their power management system. I'd prepared thoroughly: requirements documents, test data, clear specifications.

Fifteen minutes in, their lead engineer said, "Your power draw assumptions seem optimistic. We're seeing different numbers in our testing."

I bristled. We'd validated those assumptions extensively. "Our test data shows we're well within the specified range," I responded, perhaps more sharply than necessary. "What methodology are you using for your measurements?"

The pause spoke volumes. When he responded, his voice shifted from collaborative to defensive. "We're using the same test protocols that we've used successfully on three previous programs."

I realized I had questioned his competence in front of his team, though he was only complaining about our data. I completely missed what happened behind the words. While I focused on the technical architecture of our interface, I completely ignored the emotional undercurrents of the conversation—the trust and psychological safety that would determine whether we could collaborate effectively.

Origin Story:
Learning to See Beyond the Technical

My education in reading the room began two decades earlier when I worked in the commercial satellite industry, meeting with customers and colleagues from around the world. Until then, I'd mostly worked with other American engineers who shared similar communication styles, professional expectations, and cultural references. We might disagree on technical approaches, but we generally operated from the same underlying framework of how business conversations were supposed to work.

My work in commercial satellites changed all that. Now, I was in meetings with engineers from Europe, Asia, South America, and the Middle East. Each collaboration brought different technical perspectives and entirely different approaches to communication, hierarchy, conflict, and decision-making.

Effective emotional architecture must be designed for different cultural contexts. Just as technical systems need different specifications for different operating environments, emotional systems need different design parameters for the varied cultural approaches to authority, directness, and consensus-building.

I learned to draw information out of people who felt too shy to share their concerns directly. I discovered how to redirect people who were eager to share and dominated the conversation. I practiced driving discussions toward consensus when the participants brought very different ideas about what consensus even looked like.

I recognized people were showing up with their own contextual pressures that had nothing to do with the technical challenge we were supposedly solving. This was revelatory. I'd spent my entire career thinking that engineering discussions were about engineering. Engineering discussions are about *people* discussing engineering. That makes them infinitely more complex.

My global experience taught me to look at my American colleagues through a more empathetic lens, too. Everyone brings their own context, pressures, and perspectives to technical discussions, even when we think we're all speaking the same language.

The Technical Leader's Blind Spot

Let me bring you back to the present to see how those global lessons show up in my current work. After leaving commercial satellites, I moved into the human spaceflight business, where I have worked for two decades. Without the global context, I easily shifted back into the American-centric approach to group dynamics and walked into technical meetings thinking my job was simple: present the data, explain the logic, and make the engineering case. If people disagreed, it was because they didn't understand the technical facts. If they seemed resistant, they needed better explanations.

Going back to the call with our supplier about power management shows how I was missing the most important point. While I focused on interface specifications and requirement documents, an entirely different conversation was happening in parallel. I missed the conversation about trust, respect, organizational pressures, and professional reputation. I didn't see the conversation about who held authority, whose expertise was valued, and how much risk each party was willing to absorb. I was fluent in the technical language. I was illiterate in the emotional one. In technical situations, both languages are always spoken simultaneously. It's the role of the technical leader to be fluent in both.

The Invisible Operating System

Every technical conversation has two conversations happening at once. There's the obvious one—the facts, the data, the specifications we're all supposedly focused on. That's the conversation I'd been trained to have, the one I was good at. Then there's the invisible one. The one about whether people trust each other, what they're afraid will happen if this decision goes wrong, whose reputation is on the line, and what organizational pressures are shaping how they hear what you're saying. That conversation happened whether or not I paid attention to it.

I'd spent my entire career becoming fluent in the first conversation while remaining completely illiterate in the second. It was like trying to debug a complex system while ignoring half the components.

Most technical leaders are experts at reading the first system. We can spot flawed assumptions, catch calculation errors, and identify design risks from across the room. We often operate blindly within the human system. This is the fundamental challenge that defines an Emotional Architect: mastering the simultaneous design of technical and human systems.

In that supplier call, while I focused on technical accuracy, my counterpart was navigating organizational politics I knew nothing about. While I pushed for clarity on specifications, he protected his team from what felt like scope creep.[2] While I tried to make efficient decisions, he managed invisible pressures from his management chain. The technical content was straightforward. The emotional context was incredibly complex.

Because I wasn't reading the human system, I couldn't lead the technical conversation effectively. I operated as a traditional technical leader—competent in one system, blind to the other.

---

2   Scope creep is a term used to describe what happens when a project expands beyond the original goals, requirements, or tasks. This happens when we're trying to be kind and generous and agree to add on a small task or to provide additional documentation that wasn't in the original project definition. While this seems like a good way to maintain a relationship with the customer, this additional effort doesn't come with budget or schedule, so the impact can be lower profitability or delayed deliveries.

What I needed to become was an Emotional Architect: someone who could design and navigate both systems with equal skill.

Engineering Your Observational Skills: The Foundation of Emotional Architecture

After that disaster of a call—and the uncomfortable cleanup that followed—I realized I needed to develop an entirely different set of observational skills. I needed to get better at noticing what was happening between people, not just what was happening with the technical content. Fortunately, I realized this was not an unattainable or mysterious ability; it was something I could actually learn. It was observational engineering applied to a different kind of system.

This dual-system fluency is the foundation of emotional architecture. Every skill we'll explore in this book—building trust, navigating disagreement, managing technical compromise—depends on your ability to read both the technical and human systems operating in every interaction.

Learning to See What I'd Been Missing

Over the next few months, I took notes after every difficult meeting. What did I miss? What signals should I have caught? Where did conversations go sideways without warning?

The pattern that emerged surprised me. I noticed there were always two conversations happening simultaneously: the technical one I tracked obsessively, and the emotional one I completely ignored. When I finally paid attention to both, the way I saw these challenges changed.

I saw that Maria's sudden formality during design reviews meant I'd triggered something about her expertise feeling questioned. Eric's retreat into monosyllabic responses was his way of protecting himself when he disagreed with an approach but didn't feel safe saying so. Sarah's excessive qualification of every statement (*I might be wrong, but…*) appeared when organizational pressures made her afraid of being seen as the problem. *These weren't personality quirks. They were data points about the human system under stress.*

I forced myself to track both conversations simultaneously. During technical discussions, part of my attention stayed on the engineering content while another part watched for the moments when human dynamics shifted. When did voices get tighter? Who stopped asking questions? What topics made people lean back instead of lean forward?

It took months to gain even marginal competence in this dual-system awareness. I'd catch myself so focused on proving a technical point that I'd miss obvious signs of resistance building in the room. Other times, I'd be so concerned about managing everyone's emotional state that I'd lose track of the actual engineering decisions we needed to make. Only after I realized technical skill and human awareness aren't mutually exclusive was I able to get comfortable with reading both.

The hardest patterns to catch were the unspoken constraints that everyone was navigating but no one was directly addressing. Someone might be worried about budget pressures they couldn't discuss openly. A team member might fear their expertise was being questioned. Organizational politics might make certain solutions feel too risky to propose, even when they were technically sound.

I tracked who did the emotional labor of keeping everyone comfortable. When did people suddenly defer decisions to avoid owning outcomes? What statements sounded like respectful collaboration but were subtle ways of handing me their risk while staying safely uninvolved?

The trickiest skill became knowing when to bring the focus toward the human system and shift from the technical content. Sometimes a room full of awkwardness needed technical clarity to move forward. Other times, continuing with the technical discussion was a way of avoiding the actual conversation that needed to happen.

After difficult meetings, I followed up with individuals privately, "What did I miss in there?" "How did that discussion feel from your perspective?" "What would have made that conversation more effective?" These post-meeting conversations taught me more about reading rooms than any framework could.

I consistently missed the environmental context in these interactions. I didn't notice the external pressures shaping how people showed up in our interactions. Recent organizational failures might make everyone risk-averse. Budget cuts could make every expenditure feel politically charged. Layoff rumors might cause people to protect themselves rather than collaborate openly.

Months of practicing this new awareness paid off during another high-stakes supplier meeting. This meeting brought the same level of complexity, the same mix of stakeholders, the same potential for everything to go sideways. This time felt different from the moment people joined the call.

About fifteen minutes into our technical discussion, I noticed voices tightening, pauses stretching longer, and an engaged teammate suddenly going quiet. Instead of pushing forward with the agenda, I took a risk. "It feels like we're not all in agreement on this direction. Can we pause here and make sure we're all working from the same assumptions?"

The room shifted. Someone finally admitted they were worried about the schedule impact we hadn't discussed. Another person brought up budget constraints that were hovering in the background of every decision. A third team member revealed they weren't comfortable with the risk level but didn't want to appear obstructionist by raising concerns.

Instead of us all leaving the meeting feeling like we were being pushed into a poor decision, this approach took twenty minutes of honest conversation about what constrained our choices. Only then could we have the ten-minute conversation to solve what turned out to be a much simpler technical problem than any of us realized.

I wish these were newfound telepathic powers, but it isn't that easy. Through months of work, I'd simply learned to create space for the full conversation—technical and human—instead of trying to bulldoze through resistance that was ultimately valuable information in disguise. Technical problems live within human systems. When you can see the entire system, you can engineer solutions that work for everyone involved.

The Integration Challenge: When Emotional Architecture Matters Most

The hardest part about reading both systems simultaneously is learning when to pause technical content to address human dynamics. Every technical leader faces this tension: do you push forward with the agenda, or do you stop to handle the interpersonal issues?

This is where emotional architecture becomes critical. Traditional approaches often push through human system problems, hoping technical logic will prevail. Emotional Architects understand that the human system must be functional for the technical system to work properly.

When people feel unheard, they can't engage with technical content effectively. They're spending their cognitive resources on self-protection instead of problem-solving. Addressing human dynamics isn't a distraction from technical work. It's engineering the conditions where technical excellence becomes possible.

Your job as an Emotional Architect is to design interactions where both systems can function optimally. Addressing trust issues sometimes means slowing down technical discussions. Sometimes it means acknowledging invisible pressures before diving into specifications. It can involve allowing worries to be expressed prior to making a choice. The most efficient technical discussions happen when you've designed the human system to be stable and supportive. This is the foundation that makes every other skill possible.

Digital Communication is Different

The shift to remote and hybrid work has made reading the room exponentially more challenging for technical teams. When half your team is on mute with cameras off, how do you sense when someone has a concern they're not voicing? When stakeholder meetings happen through screens and with poor audio quality, how do you pick up on the subtle tension that signals deeper organizational issues?

During the pandemic, our entire technical review process moved online. Suddenly, conversations that used to flow naturally became stilted exchanges where people talked over each other. This led to unspoken concerns and decisions lacking collaborative energy, which resulted in poor outcomes.

Sure, we lost visual cues, but the bigger issue is that digital communication strips away the informal moments where real understanding happens. No more hallway conversations after the meeting where someone admits their real concern. No more coffee break discussions where team members work through their confusion privately before bringing questions to the group. In digital spaces, everything becomes more formal, more performative, and, paradoxically, less communicative.

Virtual meetings turned my room-reading skills upside down. Everything I'd learned about tracking energy and engagement had to be rebuilt from scratch when people became tiny squares on a screen.

The audio layer became my primary diagnostic tool. I listened to what people said and how their voices changed throughout conversations. I noted when someone who usually jumped right in was taking longer pauses. I started thinking of this as the 'Latency Gap'—the human equivalent of a buffering icon. In a digital room, that three-second silence after a controversial proposal isn't just a delay; it's the sound of unvoiced resistance. Instead of filling that gap with more data, I learned to name it: *It's quiet after that last slide. Usually, that means we're either totally aligned or I've missed a major concern. Which one is it?*

Mute patterns revealed more than I expected. Some people stayed unmuted throughout discussions, signaling comfort and engagement. Others clicked mute the instant they finished speaking, often indicating they were juggling other tasks or felt less invested in the conversation. Most telling were the people who muted immediately after certain topics came up, showing a digital equivalent of physically stepping back from uncomfortable territory.

Chat behavior opened another window into what people were thinking and not vocalizing. Technical questions typed instead of spoken often meant someone didn't feel safe asking verbally. Side conversations in private messages suggested that the official discussion missed something important. Sometimes excessive jokes or emoji responses masked genuine concerns that felt too risky to voice directly.

Camera dynamics told their own story. Who turned off the video during specific discussions? Even in small windows, I could catch body language shifts. Someone positioning themselves at the edge of the frame showed they were stepping back from the conversation.

It's easier than you think to misread this silence. I once led a remote design review for a critical flight software update for Artemis. The lead engineer made an interesting presentation; their data made sense, and for forty-five minutes, the digital 'room' was perfectly quiet. I interpreted this as total alignment. I thought we were being efficient.

Two days later, a junior engineer sent me a private message: "I didn't want to say anything on the call, but I don't think the logic accounts for the edge case we saw in last month's simulation."

That was a failure of room reading. Because I hadn't designed a way for "half-formed" ideas to surface in a remote setting, the team had defaulted to the safest digital behavior: staying on mute. I had focused on the technical presentation while completely missing the audio signal that the team was merely compliant, not committed.

My core challenge was translating existing skills across completely different formats. I still looked for the same human dynamics: discomfort, disagreement, hidden constraints, unspoken concerns. The signals manifested differently.

Take detecting disagreement. In person, I'd watch for crossed arms, avoided eye contact, or side glances between team members. In virtual meetings, those same dynamics showed up as sudden camera-off behavior during controversial topics, delayed responses with visible typing indicators that started and stopped, or increased private chat activity during specific discussions.

Email presented its own minefield. Technical discussions, which could have been resolved in a ten-minute face-to-face conversation, stretched into days of back-and-forth messages, creating more confusion than clarity. I learned to watch for shorter and more formal responses over time, people suddenly dropping out of discussions, and CC lists that kept growing, a key sign signaling escalating tension no one addressed directly.

Human dynamics don't disappear in digital environments. They require different sensory channels and response techniques to navigate effectively.

Slack, Teams, and other instant messaging platforms create an illusion of casual communication that can be problematic for technical teams. The informal format makes people think they can communicate complex technical concepts quickly and easily. The real-time nature makes people feel like they're having actual conversations. They're not. What they're actually having are fragmented exchanges where context gets lost, nuance disappears, and misunderstandings compound faster than they can be corrected.

I've seen bad technical decisions made through disconnected, days-long Slack conversations that might have taken five minutes to resolve in person. Because no one took the time to make sure everyone was on the same page, the thread created days of confusion and rework. I started developing *Textual X-Ray Vision* to catch these failures before they compounded. I looked for excessive qualification—when an engineer starts a comment with *I might be wrong, but… or Correct me if I'm overthinking this…* It can seem like a technical disclaimer. More often, it's a flare gun signaling a lack of psychological safety. They are navigating a perceived threat to their expertise, and as the architect, you have to step in and stabilize the foundation before the technical discussion can move forward.

How This Shows Up Everywhere: The Social Media Amplification

Social media provides an extreme example of what happens when we lose the ability to read context entirely. Think about the comment sections of any technical post on LinkedIn. Engineers often debate implementation specifics without fully considering the constraints faced by the original poster. People critique approaches without knowing the organizational context that shaped the decision.

Platforms like X and LinkedIn often mirror technical review meetings where the focus shifts to performing expertise rather than solving problems. The format encourages responding to individual posts as if they exist in isolation, rather than recognizing that every technical discussion happens within a larger human context.

What makes this relevant to technical leadership? These same patterns show up in:

- Email chains where engineers argue past each other without understanding constraints
- Virtual meetings where people make statements instead of asking questions
- Technical reviews where everyone focuses on finding flaws rather than improving solutions
- Cross-team discussions where each group defends its approach without understanding others' pressures

The digital world has amplified our tendency to focus on looking smart rather than being useful. In technical leadership, this translates to teams that can critique each other's work brilliantly but struggle to build anything together.

The boundary principle still applies: understanding different perspectives doesn't mean accommodating every position or endlessly trying to find a middle ground. It's important that we don't lean so far into collaborative approaches that we enable destructive behavior or abandon our responsibility to maintain standards and direction. There's a difference between someone who disagrees with your technical approach and someone who's undermining the team's ability to function effectively. There's a difference between healthy debate about priorities and behavior that creates a toxic environment for others.

The skill is learning to distinguish between someone who has a different perspective worth understanding and someone who is unwilling to engage constructively. Reading the room includes recognizing when the room has become toxic—whether that's a social media thread or a technical team meeting.

The View from Outside: Understanding Hidden Pressures

Remember that cross-company call from the start of this chapter? It wasn't until much later that I learned the other company was navigating a perfect storm of organizational chaos that had nothing to do with our technical discussion.

They were in the middle of a major acquisition. Every expenditure was being scrutinized by the new management, who didn't understand the existing commitments. The engineers on our call were genuinely worried about their job security and whether their entire division would survive the reorganization.

Some of their new management already questioned whether this project should continue at all. The team members I spoke with had been told to *be more cost-conscious and justify every decision*, but hadn't received clear guidance about what that meant for ongoing commitments.

While I focused on technical specifications and delivery timelines, they were managing a completely different set of pressures: fear about their continued employment, uncertainty about decision-making authority, and the stress of trying to prove their value to managers who might eliminate their roles entirely.

The defensive responses I'd interpreted as unreasonable technical positions were people trying to protect themselves and their teams in an environment where any misstep could justify further cuts.

None of this context was visible to me during the call. I was reading only the technical system while they were primarily operating within the human system. No wonder we couldn't find common ground.

When It Goes Wrong: The Conference That Wasn't

I learned about digital-age room reading failure the hard way when I was invited to speak at what I thought was a technical conference. The topic was my leadership journey and how we can get more women into senior levels in aerospace companies. It's a topic I'm passionate about and eager to share my thoughts on (and one of the reasons I am writing this book).

This was an excellent opportunity for me to be recognized for my work in this field. The conference was at a luxurious hotel; the accommodations and conference fee were paid, and I went with a very enthusiastic outlook.

In the end, the conference turned out to be a carefully engineered sales pitch where companies could pay for access to senior leaders at major companies. The people there didn't want to hear from me about leadership development. They were looking for networking opportunities and business connections.

The lesson I learned was about applying the same observational skills to any high-stakes interaction—professional or technical. The warning signs were all there in the digital communications leading up to the event, and I completely misread them.

I missed several red flags that show up in technical contexts too:

- Email invitations were vague about the actual content (like technical meetings with unclear objectives)
- The website focused more on networking opportunities than learning outcomes (like technical reviews that emphasize stakeholder management over problem-solving)
- Pre-event surveys asked more about my company and role than my presentation topics (like technical discussions where people seem more interested in your authority than your expertise)
- No clear agenda or learning objectives were provided in advance (like technical meetings where the real purpose isn't stated upfront)

This shows up in technical leadership as:

- Vendor meetings disguised as technical consultations
- Technical reviews that are disguised as budget justification sessions
- Cross-team collaborations where one group has a hidden agenda
- Stakeholder meetings where the stated purpose doesn't match the real purpose

Whether it's a fake conference or a technical meeting with hidden agendas, the same principle applies. When the stated purpose doesn't align with behavior patterns, dig deeper before committing resources.

It wasn't all bad. I did make several connections that turned out to be beneficial. However, I totally misread that room, and now I scrutinize all professional opportunities more carefully. I've learned to pay attention to the digital breadcrumbs that reveal the true purpose behind any professional interaction.

Coaching Conversations:
The Performance Review Wake Up Call

When I worked in commercial satellites, my manager held my performance review at the end of the year, and he told me something that has stuck with me and shifted how I show up at work. He said my desire to have the answer right away hurt my credibility. This was a shock. I thought being able to respond quickly to technical questions was a strength. I prided myself on my ability to think on my feet and provide immediate analysis when stakeholders needed decisions.

What my manager helped me understand was that my rush to provide answers prevented me from reading the room effectively. I worried about how my knowing or not knowing would look to others, that I wasn't taking time to understand what was being asked or what concerns were driving the question.

Instead of taking a moment to breathe, think, and maybe even say, "Let me get back to you," I focused on performing competence rather than being competent. It's a sort of reverse room-reading where you're so focused on how others perceive you that you miss what's happening in the interaction.

This is something I still catch myself doing. The pressure to be the technical expert can override the more important skill of understanding the human dynamics that determine whether your technical expertise can be useful.

Now when someone asks me a complex technical question, I'm learning to pause and ask clarifying questions, "Help me understand what decision this analysis will inform" or "What's driving the urgency around this particular aspect?" These questions help me read both the technical and human systems before providing answers.

The Cost of Emotional Illiteracy

None of us enjoys thinking of ourselves as illiterate about anything. I was frustrated with myself for not seeing the human variable in that fateful call. I learned that being emotionally literate is a critical competency in technical work. It was a skill I needed to develop.

When technical professionals can't read the human system, the consequences ripple far beyond uncomfortable phone calls:

- Decisions get delayed because unspoken concerns never surface properly, or decisions are made based on missing information, leading to future problems.
- Innovation gets stifled because people don't feel safe proposing ideas that might be wrong.
- Quality suffers because team members stop raising questions that could prevent failures.
- Relationships deteriorate because small misunderstandings compound into major conflicts.
- Projects fail not because of technical complexity, but because of human system breakdowns.

In that supplier call, I was so focused on the technical details that I completely missed the human dynamics that were making it impossible for anyone to hear and process the technical content clearly. The aftermath took time and energy from far too many people. That slowed progress toward a solution and damaged trust between the companies.

The Emotional Architect's First Skill

Once I paid attention to both systems simultaneously, I looked at conversations differently. I saw that every technical conversation exists within an emotional container. The quality of the container determines whether technical excellence can emerge.

When people feel threatened, they protect themselves—even if that protection undermines the technical work. That's when I realized I wasn't there to be the smartest person in the room anymore. I was there to create the conditions where everyone else could be smart.

The technical problem was often the easy part. The hard part was building the emotional container that would allow the technical problem to be solved well. This meant recognizing when the human system was under stress and pausing technical discussions to address emotional dynamics: voices getting tighter, people asking fewer questions, collaboration feeling forced. It meant acknowledging the pressures people were carrying—budget concerns, schedule anxiety, organizational politics—even when they weren't explicitly stated.

I learned to create space for concerns to surface safely. Instead of rushing toward technical solutions, I built bridges across different perspectives and organizational contexts. Acknowledging that strong emotional support is essential for engineering excellence kept me from acting as a team therapist.

The shift was profound. Technical problems that had seemed intractable often dissolved once I addressed the human dynamics. Stakeholder conflicts that appeared to be about specifications turned out to be about trust and communication. Team performance issues that looked like competency gaps were psychological safety problems in disguise.

A Critical Caveat: When Good Faith Isn't Present

The techniques in this book work when everyone involved is willing to own their part in creating solutions. They assume people want to contribute to shared success, even when they disagree about methods or priorities. They're built on the foundation that most technical conflicts stem from different perspectives on the same problem, not from different intentions about solving problems.

This assumption isn't always valid.

Let's be honest: toxic personalities exist in technical environments, too. These are people who are committed to being "right" at all costs, who consistently position themselves as victims of circumstances beyond their control, or who use every conversation as an opportunity to attack rather than collaborate. They're the colleagues who take credit for successes while distancing themselves from failures, who resist developing competence in areas where someone else will do the work, and who have learned to frame their avoidance of responsibility as personality traits: "I'm just not good with details" or "I'm more of a big picture person."

Recognizing the Patterns

Toxic individuals often present well in technical environments because they can demonstrate competence in narrow areas while systematically avoiding accountability for broader outcomes. They may be brilliant individual contributors who become destructive when required to collaborate. They might be articulate advocates for "best practices" who never apply those practices to their own work when inconvenient.

Warning signs of toxic teammates include:

- Consistent patterns of blaming external circumstances for their failures while taking personal credit for successes
- Resistance to feedback that persists even when delivered skillfully and with support
- Willingness to undermine team success rather than acknowledge their own mistakes
- Strategic incompetence in areas where they want others to carry responsibility
- Retaliation against people who hold them accountable, even when done professionally

These patterns differ from normal technical disagreements or personality conflicts. They represent a fundamental unwillingness to engage in the collaborative problem-solving that complex technical work requires.

The Limitations of Emotional Architecture

No amount of emotional architecture can fix someone who refuses to participate constructively. The frameworks in this book will help you recognize toxic patterns earlier and protect yourself and your team from the damage they cause. They'll give you structured approaches for managing difficult personalities while minimizing their impact on team effectiveness. They won't transform someone who is unwilling to engage in good faith.

This is a recognition of emotional architecture's proper scope. These skills enable collaboration among people who share basic professional values, even when they disagree about technical approaches or have different working styles. They're not therapeutic interventions for personality disorders or corrective measures for intentional sabotage.

As Adam Grant observes in his research on organizational culture, "In toxic cultures, people get promoted for results even if they destroy relationships. Abuse is seen as the price of high performance. In healthy cultures, no level of individual excellence justifies undermining people. You're not a high performer if you don't elevate others."[3]

Understanding this distinction helps you recognize when you're dealing with a systems problem (people working in good faith within a dysfunctional culture) versus a people problem (individuals who are incompatible with collaborative technical work).

Your Job as an Emotional Architect

Your job as an Emotional Architect is to design and protect the emotional infrastructure that enables technical excellence. Sometimes this means recognizing when someone's behavior is actively corrupting that infrastructure—and taking action to preserve the system you've built. Most of the time, this means building trust, facilitating difficult conversations, and designing processes that bring out people's strongest contributions. Sometimes it means recognizing when someone isn't willing to work

---

3   Grant, A. (2022, March 14). "In toxic cultures, people get promoted for results even if they destroy relationships..." [LinkedIn post]. LinkedIn. https://www.linkedin.com/posts/adammgrant_in-toxic-cultures-people-get-promoted-for-activity-6909171601515110400-syCO

constructively and making the hard decisions that protect the team's ability to succeed.

This might involve:

- Setting clear boundaries about acceptable professional behavior
- Documenting patterns of problematic interactions
- Limiting toxic individuals' participation in team activities and focusing their efforts toward narrow technical areas
- Working with human resources or management to address persistent problems
- In extreme cases, removing people from teams or projects when their behavior consistently undermines collective success

These decisions require courage because toxic individuals often create just enough plausible deniability to make intervention feel harsh or unfair. They're skilled at positioning themselves as victims of "difficult" colleagues or "unreasonable" expectations. They may have allies who haven't seen the full range of their behavior.

Protecting Your Own Energy

Working with toxic personalities is emotionally exhausting, even when you have strong boundaries and clear frameworks. They consume a disproportionate amount of your attention and energy. Instead of investing in developing capable team members and advancing important technical work, you're managing your energy.

Part of emotional architecture is recognizing when to stop investing in relationships that consistently drain rather than energize you. The distinction matters: someone who's struggling or who communicates differently is worth your investment. Someone whose fundamental approach to collaboration is incompatible with the team's success is not.

You cannot architect emotional systems that function well when key participants are actively working to undermine those systems. Your responsibility is to protect the people who are working in good faith, even when that protection requires difficult decisions about people who aren't.

Reflection Framework: Developing Your Observation Skills

The goal isn't to become a mind reader, but to notice the human dynamics that either support or undermine technical conversations.

Think About Your Recent Meetings

What energy shifts did you notice that you initially ignored? Maybe someone became quiet when they'd been engaged, or the room felt more tense after a particular topic came up.

How do you currently distinguish between technical confusion and interpersonal tension? When someone asks a lot of questions, are they trying to understand the content, or are they uncomfortable with the direction?

In virtual meetings, what digital cues help you understand engagement levels? Muting patterns, camera behavior, and response timing often reveal more than words.

When technical discussions get stuck, how often is it more likely a human systems issue disguised as a technical problem?

One Thing to Try This Week

In your next important meeting, spend the first few minutes just observing the energy in the room before diving into the content. Notice who seems engaged versus guarded and see if that awareness changes how you facilitate the discussion.

Playbook: Reading and Responding to Human Systems

When You're Getting Polite Silence

This feels like you're presenting a technical proposal and getting polite nods but no real engagement or questions.

Watch for people trying to be polite rather than engaged, your presentation moving too fast for people to process, or important concerns that feel too risky to voice directly.

Pause and acknowledge what you're observing: "I'm noticing this feels pretty quiet. I want to make sure we're aligned before moving forward."

Ask directly about what you're seeing: "What questions do you have that we haven't addressed yet?"

Create space for concerns: "What would you need to see differently to feel comfortable with this approach?"

Check for understanding versus agreement: "Help me understand if this approach makes sense from your perspective."

It can be uncomfortable when you aren't getting engagement. It's difficult to read the room, so asking some questions or being direct with your audience gets you all on the same page.

When One Person Dominates the Discussion

We've been there. Someone with strong opinions is taking over technical conversations while others become increasingly quiet.

Watch out for dominators who don't realize their impact, quiet people who have important insights but feel shut out, or group dynamics where seniority or personality is overriding technical merit. Here are some ideas to include the rest of the group.

Acknowledge the contribution without endorsing it: "Thanks for that perspective. I want to hear from others before we continue."

Create explicit opportunities for other voices: "Maria, what's your take on this approach?"

Use process interventions: "Let's pause here and make sure we're hearing from everyone before we continue."

Address the pattern directly if needed: "I want to make sure we're getting input from all the expertise in the room."

Letting a single person or small group dominate means you won't get every opinion. Actively asking others to weigh in encourages quieter or more timid teammates to speak up and shows that you value perspectives beyond the loudest voices.

When Something Feels Off But You Can't Name It

The technical discussion seems normal, but your instincts are telling you something important is missing.

Watch out for your own anxiety clouding your judgment, genuine technical concerns that people feel unsafe expressing, or organizational pressures that are constraining the conversation in ways you don't see.

Trust your intuition and investigate: "It feels like we're not all agreeing about this direction. Can we slow down and make sure we're seeing the same picture?"

Ask about what's not being said: "What aren't we discussing that might be important here?"

Check for invisible constraints: "What pressures or concerns might be affecting how we think about this problem?"

Look for patterns in what's being avoided: "Are there aspects of this challenge that we keep skirting around?"

If things feel weird, it's a reminder to ask questions. You can't trust that people will speak up if they're unsure about the direction. It's uncomfortable to call people out or to take a detour during a conversation. It's better to ask the questions than to clean up the consequences of unspoken constraints.

When Virtual Meetings Feel Disconnected

Using digital communication is a primary pathway in today's interconnected world. Sometimes it can feel like your online technical discussions lack the energy and engagement of in-person conversations.

Watch for people who are multitasking rather than engaging, technical concepts that aren't translating well to a virtual format, or team members who participate differently online versus in person.

Pay attention to digital body language: camera positioning, muting patterns, chat activity, and response timing all provide information about engagement.

Create explicit check-in points: "Before we continue, I want to make sure everyone is tracking with this approach."

Use multiple channels for input: enable chat, polls, or break-out conversations to give people different ways to contribute.

Build in informal connection time: Start meetings with brief personal check-ins or leave time for casual conversation.

There are many reasons virtual meetings can feel discon-nected. It's not always possible to meet in-person but being aware of the disconnection and taking deliberate steps to improve engagement results in better awareness.

When People Avoid Difficult Topics

Are you noticing that conversations consistently steer away from challenging technical or interpersonal issues that need to be addressed?

Watch for your own tendency to avoid conflict, legitimate concerns about psychological safety in the group, or technical issues that have become politically charged.

Name the avoidance pattern: "I notice we keep changing subjects when we get to this topic. What makes it difficult to discuss?"

Create safety for difficult conversations: "This is hard to talk about, and it's important that we figure it out together."

Address the process, not just the content: "How can we have this conversation in a way that feels productive rather than threatening?"

Model vulnerability about your own concerns: "I'm worried about how this decision might affect the team dynamic. What are you seeing?"

I don't think anyone enjoys difficult conversations. As leaders, it's important to be clear with your messaging. When someone has a topic they're uncomfortable surfacing, it's your role to make space to discuss it.

When You Have a Bad-Faith Saboteur

The Bad-Faith Saboteur is a structural hazard. They do not just underperform; they actively weaponize cultural values—like psychological safety or empathy—to bypass accountability and create friction. They thrive in ambiguity because clarity creates a trail of responsibility they wish to avoid.

Watch for arguments about "process" or "feeling unsafe" that only appear when a deadline is missed or a technical error is caught. If the friction consistently serves as a smokescreen for non-performance, you are dealing with sabotage, not a misunderstanding.

Depersonalize the conflict: When they trigger a dispute, refuse the role of mediator. Re-center the conversation on the Technical Standard. "This isn't an interpersonal issue; it's a failure to meet the verification protocol. Fix the gap by Tuesday."

Create a record: Move all coordination to shared, traceable documents. Bad-faith actors rely on "he said/she said" dynamics to maintain plausible deniability. Documentation is the infrastructure that makes sabotage visible.

Stop the "rescue" cycle: If they manufacture a crisis to force you into hero mode, let the natural consequences of the system play out within a controlled range. Refuse to absorb the emotional labor of their "emergency."

When You Have a Chronic Energy Drain

The Chronic Energy Drain represents a capacity leak in your emotional infrastructure. These individuals rely on strategic helplessness to offload all initiative and emotional risk onto the leader. If every task requires an hour of your "processing power" before they start, you aren't leading—you're being used as an external CPU.

Watch for: A pattern where "I don't know how" is used as a permanent shield against taking ownership. The diagnostic test: If you stopped providing the emotional labor for this person today, would their work grind to a complete halt? If so, they aren't a contributor; they are a tax.

Enforce initiative: Stop the Coaching Loop. If they claim they "don't know how to approach" a routine task, do not provide the answer. State the expectation: "You have the documentation. I expect the final output in the status report."

Protect the foundation: A leader's energy is a finite resource. If 80% of your relational capacity is spent on one non-performer, you are effectively stealing that time from the high-performers who are actually building the system.

Accept the exit: Recognize that for some, "investing in helplessness" is a survival strategy for avoiding work. Your job isn't to fix the person, but to protect the system by isolating the drain or beginning the offboarding process. You cannot build a high-performance organization on a foundation of people who refuse to carry their own bricks.

The Beginning of Wisdom

Looking back at that call, I could finally see what I'd missed. What started as a routine technical discussion about interface requirements had escalated to director-level involvement because I'd completely missed the human context—the acquisition pressures, job insecurity, and organizational chaos that was driving the defensive responses. That experience taught me something important about technical leadership. Technical problems live within human systems. You cannot solve the technical problem without first understanding the human context it exists within.

This doesn't mean every technical discussion needs to become a therapy session. It means developing the skill to identify when human dynamics are blocking technical progress—and knowing how to address the human dynamics so that technical excellence can emerge.

In the chapters ahead, we'll build your toolkit for navigating these human systems skillfully:

- Having difficult conversations that strengthen rather than damage relationships
- Deciding when both technical and emotional factors are in play
- Preventing conflicts before they derail important work
- Building teams that feel safe enough to be technically excellent

It all starts here: learning to read the room. Learning to see what people are saying and what they're experiencing. Learning to recognize when the human system needs your attention before the technical system can function properly. The most elegant technical solutions in the world are worthless if the human system isn't equipped to implement them.

The next time you walk into a technical review, a design meeting, or a cross-functional planning session, try this: spend the first few minutes reading both systems. Notice what's happening technically and notice what's happening emotionally. You might be surprised by how much more you can see once you look for both.

Why Trust Comes Next

Reading the room taught me to see the invisible dynamics that shape every technical conversation. I could now detect when someone was uncomfortable, when organizational pressures were creating defensiveness, and when cultural differences were causing misunderstandings.

Observation alone wasn't enough. Knowing your colleague was stressed about job security during an acquisition didn't automatically solve the problem. Recognizing that someone felt their expertise was being questioned didn't instantly create better collaboration. Seeing the human dynamics clearly was only the first step.

The next challenge was learning how to respond to what I was seeing—how to create the psychological safety and credibility that would allow people to show up as their best selves, even under pressure. That meant building something that had to be earned over time: trust.

Building Trust:
When You're the Outsider

Chapter 3

L ET ME TAKE you back to how this all began. Three months before my colleague sent me his resignation email, I'd been assigned to lead what everyone quietly called the 'difficult' team.

I could feel them watching me. Not openly—these were skilled technicians, too professional for obvious skepticism. I caught the glances. The careful politeness. The way conversations shifted when I walked into the high bay. The subtle resistance wrapped in compliance.

I was an outsider. The engineer from Denver who dropped into their world at Kennedy Space Center to lead a project. None of them asked for my help. I did things differently than they were used to. I asked questions that challenged their standard procedures. Worst of all, I asked them to own their part of the work in ways they'd never been expected to do before. They didn't trust me. Honestly, I couldn't blame them.

What made it worse was that I could feel their doubt creeping into my confidence. Every time someone responded to my suggestions with barely concealed skepticism, a voice in my head whispered: *Maybe they're right. Maybe you don't belong here. Maybe you're in over your head.*

I represented a risk to people who'd built their reputations on following established processes. As a contractor in a world of direct employees, I didn't know their history, their informal networks, or the unspoken rules that governed how things got done.

If that weren't challenging enough, I was also fighting a trust battle on another front. The managers that I reported to questioned my approach. They were unhappy with the fact that I was a subcontractor. This made them concerned I wasn't following the usual dynamics of the on-site team. I was a rogue element in a system that valued predictability. I had eleven months to build something that had never been built before. I couldn't do it alone.

Origin Story:
Learning What Trust Costs

Being a woman in engineering means learning what trust costs before you even understand what trust is. When I first started working for Martin Marietta in 1997, I was the only woman engineer on my team at the field site. There were more women on the program, but locally, I was the "only" one in every room. I stayed later than everyone else, delivering results sooner than required, and having answers ready before anyone asked the questions.

I had to be more than competent. I had to be undeniably excellent before I could even be considered capable. This probably led to the performance feedback I received later about wanting to have answers immediately. I'd trained myself to believe that any hesitation would be interpreted as incompetence.

It was important for me to show that I could do the work and that I could do it so well that I'd be welcomed rather than simply tolerated. That pattern burned me out and stole the hours I would have spent on the things I loved.

I was unknowingly building trust based on performance, not relationships. I earned acceptance through excellence. I learned through a lot of trial and error that I wasn't building the kind of trust that could weather the inevitable moments when I didn't have all the answers.

The Trust Deficit Reality

When most professionals in technical roles step into new positions, they inherit a baseline level of trust. Maybe not deep trust, but at least the assumption that they belong there, that someone in authority believed they were qualified.

In this situation, I had none of that. Walking into that high bay for the first time, I felt like an imposter wearing credentials everyone could see right through. Eric, Maria, Tom, and Sarah looked at me and saw an unknown quantity. Someone who might disrupt their carefully developed expertise. Someone who might blame them if things went wrong. Someone who might not understand the real constraints they worked within every day. The worst part was that their skepticism made me question everything I thought I knew about guiding technical teams.

I'd been successful in Denver. I had a track record of solving complex technical problems. None of that mattered here, in this room, with these people who had no reason to believe I was anything more than another engineer with theories about how things should work.

Standing in that high bay, watching their polite skepticism, I realized nobody was going to hand me their trust just because I had the right title or the right credentials. I had to earn it, one conversation at a time, one small decision after another, one moment of proving that I saw them as people rather than resources. Earning it requires understanding what trust means to technical people—which turned out to differ greatly from what I expected.

What Trust Costs

I thought earning trust would be about proving my technical competence. I discovered that trust in technical environments is less about what you know and more about what you do when you don't know. It's about how you handle uncertainty, how you respond to someone challenging your authority, and how you treat people when things go wrong.

The first real test came three weeks in, when Eric questioned one of my technical recommendations in front of the entire team. Not aggressively, but clearly. He thought my approach would create integration problems downstream. Every instinct I had screamed to defend my position. To pull rank. To prove I was right. To show that he had missed something. The voice in my head shouted, *If you don't establish authority now, you'll never get it back.* Something held me back. Maybe it was exhaustion from constantly trying to prove myself. Maybe it was the realization that I didn't know everything about this environment that they'd been working with for years.

I took a slow, deep breath, maybe two. I could feel the heat of defensiveness drain from my mind, and instead of defending, I got curious. "Tell me more about what you're seeing. What integration problems are you worried about?"

The room went quiet. I could feel everyone watching to see how this would play out.

Eric explained his concerns. You know what? He was right about two of them and had identified a risk I hadn't considered. That moment of vulnerability—admitting I hadn't thought of something—did more to build trust than any display of technical brilliance could have.

The Emotional Labor of Being Doubted

No one tells you how emotionally exhausting it is to earn trust as an outsider. Every conversation requires extra energy to overcome baseline skepticism. Every suggestion gets filtered through their assumption that you don't understand their situation. Every mistake gets magnified as evidence that the team's initial doubts were justified.

I went home every night in those first few weeks feeling drained in a way that had nothing to do with the technical challenges. It was the constant emotional work of proving I belonged, of fighting through resistance to get basic cooperation, of maintaining confidence when they met everything I said with polite yet unmistakable doubt.

There were nights I lay awake wondering if I should just follow their established procedures instead of pushing for changes I thought would improve outcomes. It would have been so much easier to fit in than to lead change.

I also knew that if I abandoned my technical judgment to be liked, I'd lose their respect anyway. They didn't need another person to rubber-stamp their existing approach. They needed someone who could see possibilities they couldn't see. I knew this would work only if I could earn the credibility to suggest those possibilities.

Context Matters

During one of our morning coffee meetings, Maria asked a question that revealed a crucial gap in my leadership. Early in my career, I'd learned that people need to understand the purpose behind their work, not just the tasks themselves. Now Maria showed me I'd forgotten that lesson entirely.

"Why are we building this thing anyway? I mean, I know it's a test vehicle, but what's it actually going to prove?" That question revealed the first major trust barrier I needed to address: they didn't understand why their work mattered. That failure was entirely on me.

For weeks, I'd been focused on the how: procedures, schedules, technical specifications. I'd never given them the why. They were executing tasks without understanding the larger mission context that made those tasks meaningful.

The shame of this realization hit me hard. Here I was, worried about proving my technical competence, while completely failing at one of the most basic aspects of leadership: helping people understand how their work is connected to something larger than their individual assignments.

So, I stopped talking about procedures and started talking about the mission. I explained how this test vehicle would prove that our rocket could survive the journey into space. How the data we collected would inform design decisions for future missions. How their specific expertise (Eric's mechanical intuition, Maria's attention to detail, Tom's risk assessment, Sarah's probing questions) was essential to the mission's success.

I showed them how their work connected to astronaut safety, to mission objectives, and to the larger vision of human space exploration. I gave them ownership of something bigger than their individual tasks. They owned the mission rather than completing their assignments.

This taught me that trust is about showing people that their contribution matters in ways that extend beyond immediate task completion. When people understand why their expertise is essential to something meaningful, they invest themselves differently in the work and in the relationship with you as their leader.

The context conversation became the foundation for everything else that followed. Not because it was a grand gesture, but because it demonstrated that I saw them as partners in something important rather than resources to be used.

How This Shows Up Everywhere: The Universal Outsider Experience

The same trust-building principles I learned with that technical team turned out to be universal human principles. Applying them required the same kind of emotional vulnerability in every context, whether I was standing in a cleanroom or sitting at my kitchen table.

People trust you when they understand why their contribution matters. Whether it's a teenager helping with household responsibilities or a friend participating in group activities, context creates meaning, and meaning creates investment. You must be willing to share the larger purpose, even when it makes you vulnerable to having that purpose questioned or dismissed. Sometimes, your plan isn't the right path. It's okay to change after getting input that contradicts or refines your beliefs. It's always more difficult to start with a clean sheet than to edit, so being open to discussion helps your team rise to the same commitment to success you're trying to develop.

People trust you when you genuinely value their expertise. My kids became more willing to share their perspectives when I stopped treating their ideas as cute and treated them as insights worth considering. That required me to change my plans sometimes based on their input, which meant admitting I didn't always know what was best. This created a new, deeper relationship with them. By taking their inputs seriously, they learned to offer their preferences and needs upfront, which offloaded some of the emotional labor from me and built investment in our relationship.

People trust you when you give them ownership rather than assignments. Friends felt more invested in group plans when I asked for their input rather than announcing decisions. That meant accepting that the plans might not be exactly what I would have chosen, and that someone else's mistakes would affect outcomes I cared about. As a leader, you know you have reached a new level of team building when people provide genuine input rather than deferring to *whatever you think is best*.

Trust is built through consistent small actions, not grand gestures. Daily coffee conversations mattered more than any single inspirational speech. Those daily conversations required showing up consistently, even when I was tired or frustrated or would rather get to work. John Gottman's[4] research on relationships shows that trust is built through what he calls "bids for connection": small, everyday moments when people reach out and either receive a response or don't. The same principle applies to leadership: trust accumulates through

---

4   Gottman, J. M. (1999). *The Marriage Clinic: A Scientifically Based Marital Therapy*. W. W. Norton & Company.

countless micro-interactions where you either show up for people or you don't.

Amy Edmondson's[5] research on psychological safety reveals why these moments matter so much in technical environments. She found that "psychological safety is a belief that one can speak up without risk of punishment or humiliation." In her studies of high-performing teams, those with psychological safety were 47% more likely to report errors before they became problems, 27% more likely to suggest improvements, and 76% more likely to engage in the kind of creative problem-solving that technical challenges require.

When I considered these principles, I could create the conditions where technical excellence could emerge. When Eric felt safe to question my assumptions, when Maria could point out potential problems, when Tom could voice concerns without being labeled negative, we weren't just building trust. We were building the foundation for better technical outcomes.

This dynamic is just as critical in our most intimate spaces. Just as Eric or Maria needed to know their "bids" would be met with professional respect, Gottman's research shows that lasting trust in romantic relationships comes from partners who consistently turn toward each other's bids for connection rather than turning away or against them. The strongest relationships are built on a foundation of these small, daily interactions where both people feel seen and heard, not on dramatic gestures or perfect communication. Trust develops when someone can be vulnerable and knows their partner will respond with curiosity and care rather than defensiveness or the need to immediately fix or solve.

---

5   Edmondson, A. (1999). Psychological safety and learning behavior in work teams. *Administrative Science Quarterly*, 44(2), 350-383.

In professional settings outside of my immediate team, I learned trust often comes from admitting what you don't know rather than pretending to know everything. Colleagues trusted my judgment more when I was transparent about the limits of my expertise. Charles Feltman's[6] research on workplace trust helped me understand why this approach was so effective. Most of us focus primarily on demonstrating competence—showing that we have the knowledge and skills to handle technical challenges. This is necessary but insufficient for building the kind of trust that enables collaboration during conflict or uncertainty.

What Feltman calls "reliability"—keeping your agreements and doing what you say you will do—often gets misinterpreted in technical environments as having all the answers immediately. Real reliability means being honest about what you do and don't know, making realistic commitments about what you can learn or deliver, and following through consistently on those commitments.

When I said things like, "I don't have enough information to be confident about this, but here's what I can commit to learning by Thursday," my credibility increased rather than decreased. People trusted my assessments were realistic rather than optimistic, my timelines were achievable rather than aspirational, and my uncertainties were genuine rather than strategic.

Feltman describes sincerity as meaning what you say and saying what you mean. For technical leaders, this often means being willing to admit when people's considerations are just as important as technical considerations—and that you're still learning how to balance both effectively.

---

6   Feltman, C. (2009). T*he Thin Book of Trust: An Essential Primer for Building Trust at Work.* Thin Book Publishing.

This foundation became crucial when I encountered situations where someone's words about growth and collaboration were perfectly calibrated, but their actions revealed something entirely different. Understanding Feltman's framework helped me recognize that trust requires alignment across all four domains. Technical competence alone could never compensate for failures in care, reliability, or sincerity.

When It Goes Wrong: Words Don't Match Actions

The framework I'd learned about authentic trust-building was put to the test in a situation that had nothing to do with engineering—and everything to do with recognizing when someone has learned the language of growth without developing the actual capacity for it.

I had an extended conversation with a man who was interested in building a relationship with me. He said all the right things. He told me he'd been in therapy to work through his last breakup; he'd been working on his ability to be emotionally present, and he was far more evolved than his peers when it came to emotional intelligence. His words captivated me. The language was perfectly on target and even mirrored some of the very concepts I'd recently journaled. It was almost too good to be true. As it turned out, it was.

While his words were about growth and emotional intelligence, his actions consistently showed someone who wasn't ready for the vulnerability that real intimacy requires. He could articulate concepts about emotional intelligence with impressive fluency. He couldn't practice them when it mattered.

For example, when we disagreed about plans or routines, he wouldn't engage in a real dialogue. Instead of listening with curiosity, he would shut down or use therapeutic buzzwords like "you're not holding space for me" to deflect from the issue at hand. He could describe what healthy communication looked like in theoretical terms, but when pressed on inconsistencies between his stated values and his behavior, he would pivot to more sophisticated language rather than acknowledging the gap.

He had learned the vocabulary of personal development without developing the actual emotional skills. He could perform emotional literacy without being emotionally literate. Using Feltman's framework, he showed apparent competence in the language of growth while failing completely in the reliability and sincerity domains. He said he would do emotional work he wasn't willing to do and meaning something different from what his words suggested.

This experience taught me something crucial about trust: people can say all the right things about collaboration and development without being willing to do the vulnerable work.

- They can advocate for inclusivity while consistently interrupting women or junior engineers in meetings.
- They can talk about psychological safety while rolling their eyes or retaliating against people who bring up legitimate concerns when it's inconvenient.
- They can claim to value professional development while hoarding interesting assignments and shielding information from peers.

I'm not asking you to become cynical about people's words or to dismiss genuine attempts at growth. Pay attention to the alignment between what people say and what they do, especially under pressure. Trust is built through consistent action over time, not through perfect articulation of the right principles. When someone consistently demonstrates competence in talking about emotional intelligence while failing to demonstrate reliability or sincerity in practicing it, that's valuable information about their actual capacity for the collaborative work that technical leadership requires.

The pattern recognition skills that matter most in leadership show up the same way they do in relationships: trust is built through the alignment between stated values and consistent behavior, especially when nobody is watching.

In my personal relationships, I ignored the action patterns because I was so attracted to the stated intentions. In technical situations, I learned to watch for team members who say they're committed but consistently miss deadlines, colleagues who express support for collaboration but always find reasons why other people's ideas won't work, managers who claim to value innovation but punish every failure.

The painful lesson from my personal experience helped me become a better technical leader. Trust isn't built through impressive statements about your values. It's built through boring consistency in small actions that prove those values are real.

Coaching Conversations: Supporting Others Who Don't Fit

One of the most rewarding aspects of my role has been mentoring other women in technical fields, particularly those who are navigating the challenge of being outsiders in male-dominated environments.

I remember a conversation with a brilliant engineer who struggled with the same pattern I'd experienced. She worked twice as hard to prove herself while watching less qualified male colleagues advance more quickly. She was exhausted from the constant pressure to be perfect and frustrated by the emotional labor of managing other people's discomfort with her presence in technical circles.

"I feel like I can never be good enough," she told me. "I have to be exceptional, and even then, people question whether I really know what I'm talking about."

I shared with her something I wish someone had told me earlier: the goal isn't to make everyone comfortable with your presence. The goal is to build trust with the people who matter while protecting your energy from those who are committed to misunderstanding you.

I've helped emerging leaders distinguish between people who are genuinely curious about different perspectives and people who are testing whether you belong. The first group is worth investing in. The second group will exhaust you if you let them.

The coaching conversations that matter most aren't about teaching technical skills—these women are already technically excellent. They're about helping people recognize their own worth, set appropriate boundaries, and build alliances with others who value what they bring rather than constantly justifying their right to be in the room.

The View from Outside: What Others Were Seeing

In the early weeks at Kennedy Space Center, I navigated more skepticism than I had initially realized. People were polite, professional, and seemingly supportive of my unconventional approach. What I didn't know was that behind the scenes, emails were circulating about whether someone needed to get me "under control" before we had a major incident. The feedback was that my team and I were "running around like cowboys" without proper oversight.

I still have some of those emails, and I read them occasionally as a reminder that just because I have a plan doesn't mean others understand or agree with it. What felt like adaptive problem-solving to me looked like chaos to people who valued predictable processes.

My team was watching me carefully to see if I was another leader who would promise partnership and deliver micromanagement. They'd been burned before by managers who talked about valuing their input and then ignored their suggestions or implemented changes without explanation.

To my management, I represented a risk they couldn't quite quantify. They were used to contractors who came in, followed established procedures, and delivered predictable results. My approach felt chaotic to them, even when it worked. They saw me spending time on coffee conversations and team building when they wanted to see me focused on technical deliverables.

To other engineering groups, I was an unknown factor who might set precedents they didn't want to follow. If my team-centric approach succeeded, it might create pressure for them to change their own management styles.

When I looked at my approach through management's eyes, I saw that emotional architecture often looks chaotic from the outside, even when it's working. The coffee conversations and team building that felt essential to me looked like time-wasting to people who valued predictable processes. This taught me that part of being an emotional architect is accepting that your methods will be questioned until your results speak for themselves.

Choosing "trust from below" over "trust from above" came at a cost: months of organizational discomfort and second-guessing.

The payoff was an approach that worked so well that management wanted to spread it throughout the organization.

I'd learned that you must be willing to be misunderstood in the short term to build something valuable in the long term.

Building Authentic Trust Versus Artificial Hierarchy

A few weeks into those coffee conversations, I thought I had made real progress with my team. Then Maria said something during a design review, and I froze. *Wait…what did you say?* Maria spoke up and said, "You're the expert. Whatever you think."

I wasn't sure what to think. At first, I was relieved. Finally, they were showing respect for my authority! They were deferring to my expertise!

As I thought about it more, I realized I hadn't built genuine trust; I'd accidentally created a system where people felt safer deferring to authority than engaging their expertise. Real emotional architecture enables people to contribute their thinking, which deepens their compliance.

When Maria said, "You're the expert; whatever you think is best," about a procedure she had more hands-on experience with than I did, I finally got it.

I stopped the conversation. "I need your thinking on this. You've done this assembly more times than anyone else in the room. What concerns do you have about this approach?"

There was a long pause. Then Maria said, "Well, if you really want to know, I think this step might cause problems because the cable routing gets very tight when you do it that way." Now we had uncovered what real trust looks like versus what self-protection disguised as trust looks like.

Real trust meant Maria was willing to be vulnerable with me—to share her concerns, admit her perspective, and offer her expertise even when she wasn't certain I wanted to hear it. Self-protection meant avoiding vulnerability by handing me all the decision-making responsibility.

Learning to Read the Signals

Over the following weeks, I paid attention to the difference between people who genuinely trusted me and people who were protecting themselves by deferring to my authority.

When Eric trusted me, he'd say things like, "I'm worried about this approach because of what happened on the last build," or "What if we considered doing the integration in a different sequence?" He was willing to own his part of the thinking, the questions, and even the mistakes.

When Tom protected himself, he'd say, "Whatever you think is best," or "You're the expert," or "Just tell us what to do." He wanted me to own the decisions so he could avoid the risk of being wrong.

The trust-builders were willing to be wrong with me. The self-protectors wanted me to be wrong alone if things didn't work out.

The Sarah Situation

Sarah presented the biggest challenge because her self-protection was wrapped in what sounded like deep respect for my expertise.

"I value your technical judgment," she'd say, then deflect every attempt I made to get her input. "I know you'll make the right decision."

It took me weeks to learn that Sarah had been burned by a previous leader who'd asked for her input on a design decision, then blamed her when the approach didn't work. Her deference was learned self-preservation.

I had to create different conditions that made vulnerability feel safer for Sarah. Instead of asking open-ended questions like, "What's your take on this?" I started with more specific requests. "I need your expertise on this thermal analysis piece" or "Help me understand what you're seeing from the materials perspective." By creating conditions where Sarah could choose to engage authentically rather than defensively, I helped her share instead of feeling vulnerable.

When I Made Deference Impossible

When I made it impossible for people to defer decisions back to me, I felt a change in how people interacted. It wasn't an overnight fix. In the high-stakes, fast-paced environment of technical development, the instinct is always to move quickly, and the fastest way to move is to issue a directive. Stopping the conversation to force people to think for themselves felt inefficient and uncomfortable. I had to fight the urge to just say, "Here is the answer," and instead hold the space of uncertainty.

When someone said, "Whatever you think is best," I'd respond with, "I need your thinking first. What concerns do you have about each option?"

When someone said, "You're the expert," I'd say, "I need your expertise too. What would you recommend and why?"

When someone said, "I trust your judgment," I'd reply, "That means a lot, and I also need your judgment on this. What's your take?"

By refusing to be the sole oracle of the technical truth, I was shifting the psychological load back to where it belonged: the engineers holding the hardware. This forced a new kind of accountability. It sent a clear signal that I valued their minds more than their agreement. I learned to distinguish between people who needed more time and evidence that their input was valued, versus people who needed explicit permission to disagree or challenge my thinking.

Understanding When Protection Made Sense

I also discovered that self-protection sometimes signaled larger organizational dynamics that needed attention. When Tom consistently avoided ownership, I remembered he'd been asked to take ownership of projects before, then had his leader micromanage the outcome so he couldn't lead. When Sarah deflected technical discussions, it was because she'd learned that being wrong had serious consequences.

In these cases, pushing harder for vulnerability would have been counterproductive. The solution was to address the underlying conditions that made self-protection feel necessary. This meant demonstrating through my own actions that shared ownership meant shared credit and shared responsibility. When our assembly procedure worked well, I made sure everyone knew it was because of Maria's cable routing insight. When we had to modify an approach, I framed it as our collective learning rather than someone's mistake.

Building the Foundation for Real Trust

Real trust requires creating an emotional infrastructure where people feel safe to be imperfect, to learn, and to take appropriate risks. This is about designing the conditions where technical excellence can emerge. If your organizational culture punishes mistakes harshly, or if previous managers have broken trust, you may need to rebuild those conditions before authentic collaboration becomes possible.

The foundation of trust reaches beyond the personal connection to one that is more structural. Sometimes building trust means changing the systems that make trust feel dangerous. For our team, this meant establishing new norms: welcoming questions, believing mistakes were learning opportunities, and knowing good ideas could come from anyone, regardless of title or experience level. It took months of consistent behavior before people believed these norms were real, but once they did, the quality of our technical work improved dramatically.

The team that had been labeled as "difficult" became the team that other groups wanted to emulate—not because they stopped having opinions, but because they learned to share those opinions constructively.

The Management Trust Battle

Three weeks into my coffee-conversation approach with the team, my director pulled me into his office. The look on his face told me this wasn't going to be a congratulatory chat about my innovative mentoring techniques.

My director was getting nervous about our cowboy approach. "I need to see more structure," he told me during one of our weekly check-ins. "The other teams have clear hierarchies, defined roles, documented processes. Your team seems to make it up as they go."

He wasn't wrong. We *were* making it up as we went along. What looked like chaos from above was me setting up an emotional system where the team could think together and execute orders. I was designing conditions for collaborative intelligence, not individual compliance.

The emails from management during this period were telling:

- "Need to see more control over the day-to-day activities"
- "Concerned about the lack of traditional project management structure"
- "Other stakeholders are questioning whether this approach is scalable"

The trust paradox was real. The very approaches that were building trust with my team were eroding confidence from management, who valued predictability over innovation.

I asked my team to trust me with their professional reputations while my own professional reputation was under scrutiny from above. I encouraged them to take ownership and make decisions, while management questioned whether I had sufficient control over the team.

The pressure was immense. Every day brought the temptation to revert to more traditional command-and-control approaches that would satisfy management expectations. It would have been so much easier to implement clear hierarchies, documented approval processes, and regular status reporting that proved I was "managing" the team.

I'd seen what traditional approaches produced: compliance without creativity, execution without innovation, task completion without genuine investment.

I had to choose: trust from above or trust from below. I chose the team. It was the right call, but it led to months of constant second-guessing from management. I absorbed criticism about my "unconventional" methods. I endured skeptical questions about whether our approach was sustainable or scalable.

The payoff came when we delivered results that exceeded expectations, while other teams using traditional approaches struggled with the same challenges. Management's tune changed when they saw what was possible when teams owned their work and completing assignments felt effortless.

After the flight test, my director pulled me aside and said, "I'll be honest, I wasn't sure about your methods. I've been watching the other programs, and they're all asking how they can work with your team. Whatever you're doing differently, it's working."

The vindication felt good, but the real message is that building trust sometimes requires being willing to risk trust in other areas. Leading change means accepting that not everyone will understand or approve of your methods until they see the results.

The Long Game of Trust

Trust isn't built in a meeting or established through a single conversation. It accrues slowly, through countless small interactions where you prove you see people clearly, value their contributions, and can be counted on to act with their best interests in mind.

Trust, once earned, becomes incredibly resilient if you continue to act in alignment with your values and remain an emotionally safe person. The team that had initially doubted my every suggestion eventually became my strongest advocates. When other groups questioned our approach, they defended it. When management pushed back on our methods, they provided examples of why those methods worked.

The trust we built was tested repeatedly throughout that project. There were technical setbacks, schedule pressures, and budget constraints. There were moments when my decisions didn't work out as planned, when the team had to work extra hours because of my mistakes, and when the pressure from management made everyone nervous. Because we'd built trust through vulnerability, those challenges strengthened our relationship rather than weakening it.

When we delivered a flawless test flight on schedule, management's concerns about my unorthodox approach more or less evaporated. Success created trust in places where compliance never could have. For me, the real victory was watching Eric, Maria, Tom, and Sarah transform from a group of people who were written off as "difficult" into a team that other groups wanted to emulate. They went beyond building a test vehicle. They'd built themselves into leaders.

Reflection Framework: Assessing Your Trust Foundation

Trust for technical leaders is about creating conditions where people feel safe to bring their real thinking, including when they disagree with you.

Consider Your Current Team Dynamics

When people defer decisions to you, are they genuinely seeking your expertise, or are they avoiding the emotional work of taking a position? There's a big difference between "I'd value your input on this" and "whatever you think is best."

Do team members feel safe disagreeing with you, or do they default to agreement? Real trust shows up when smart people can push back on your ideas without worrying about damaging the relationship.

How do you handle being wrong? Your response to mistakes—both your own and the mistakes of others—teaches people whether intellectual honesty is valued or just claimed.

What unspoken rules or cultural dynamics might you be missing that affect how people respond to your leadership? Sometimes trust issues aren't about you personally; they're about organizational history or cultural patterns you haven't recognized.

One Thing to Try This Week

The next time someone brings you a problem, resist the urge to solve it immediately. Instead, ask, "What solutions have you already considered?" and "What would you try if I weren't available to help?" Notice both their response and your own internal reaction to stepping back from the expert role.

Playbook:
Building Trust as an Outsider

When You Face New Team Skepticism

You've joined a new team! The first thing you notice is that people are polite but clearly waiting to see if you're competent before they engage.

Watch out for the urge to prove yourself too quickly, trying to counteract specific past experiences with outsiders that went badly, or disproving skepticism about your role rather than your competence.

Acknowledge your outsider status directly: "I know I'm new here and need to earn your trust."

Ask questions that show you value their expertise: "Help me understand how you've been handling this process."

Deliver on small commitments consistently: "I said I'd get back to you by Friday with that information."

Be vulnerable about what you don't know: "I haven't worked with this system before. What should I be aware of?"

It takes time and experience for a team and its leader to feel out the interaction before they trust each other. Open, clear communication and curiosity are the fastest way to get there.

When Management Questions Your Trust-Building Approach

Sometimes you're building trust with your team using methods that make your management uncomfortable with your "unconventional" leadership style.

Watch for your approach genuinely not fitting the organizational culture, management having valid concerns you're not seeing, or the conflict affecting your team's confidence in you.

Be transparent about your methods: "Here's why I'm doing things this way and what results I expect."

Document your successes: "Here's what we've accomplished using this collaborative approach."

Find allies in management: "Who else believes in developing people's capabilities rather than managing them?"

Stay committed to your values while being strategic: "I'm happy to explain my methods, but I won't compromise on treating people with respect."

Trust in your management is as important as trust within your team. You're seeing a consistent message here with clear communication and consistency.

When Someone Keeps Testing Your Competence

It's frustrating when a team member continues to challenge your technical decisions or question your authority in ways that feel like testing rather than genuine technical disagreement.

Watch for your own defensive reactions making the situation worse, legitimate technical concerns disguised as authority testing, or organizational dynamics that are encouraging the challenging behavior.

Address the pattern directly: "I notice you seem to have concerns about my technical approach. Can we talk about what's driving that?"

Acknowledge their expertise: "You clearly have strong technical opinions. Help me understand your perspective on this."

Set boundaries around the testing: "I welcome technical disagreements, but I need them to be about the work, not about proving competence."

Look for the underlying concern: "What would you need to see from me to feel confident in this technical direction?"

When people question your competence, it's easy to get defensive. That's going to increase the tension between you. Learn to step back, evaluate their concerns, and be curious about how to move forward.

When Your Different Background Creates Distance

When you are a leader coming from a different background or company, this can create barriers to connection with your team.

Watch out for assuming your previous experience is automatically relevant, coming across as judging their current methods, or missing cultural nuances that affect how your background is perceived.

Use your differences as learning opportunities: "I've worked in different environments. What should I understand about how things work here?"

Find common ground through shared technical interests: "What projects have you worked on that you're most proud of?"

Be curious about their expertise: "I'm interested in how you've approached these types of problems in the past."

Share your experience without claiming it's better: "In my previous role, we handled this differently. What advantages do you see in your current approach?"

The experiences you've had led you to this role, in the same way that your team arrived here. It's important to recognize these differences, how they play out in your work, and how you can leverage them to be more successful. Clear communication without accusation or dismissal builds trust that bridges the divide.

Trust Enables Successful Conflict

Trust is the foundation; it's not the destination. Once you've established that people can count on you to see them clearly and act with their interests in mind, you'll inevitably face situations where smart, well-intentioned people disagree about important technical decisions.

In the next chapter, we'll explore how to navigate those disagreements skillfully—how to have difficult conversations that strengthen relationships rather than damaging them, and how to find solutions that serve the mission even when people start from very different positions.

Trust without the ability to work through conflict is fragile trust. Real trust gets tested when the stakes are high and the answers aren't obvious. That's when you discover whether you've built something that can withstand the pressure of real technical leadership challenges.

When Smart People Disagree:
The War Inside Your Head

Chapter 4

THE NUMBERS LOOKED terrible.

Sitting in my office, staring at the spreadsheet on my screen, I could see why Beck, a senior leader from central engineering was concerned. We had an alarming number of open nonconformance reports—the kind of paperwork that documents when hardware doesn't meet specifications. To anyone looking at the raw numbers, it painted a picture of a program in trouble.

I knew the context behind those numbers. When you factored in the complexity of our system, the percentage of nonconformances wasn't out of line with similar programs. More importantly, none of the open issues represented safety risks or mission-critical problems. They were mostly documentation cleanup and minor process improvements.

Our senior quality assurance leader didn't see it that way. For weeks, Beck had been pressuring my already overtaxed engineers to drop their current design work and focus on closing out the nonconformance paperwork. She'd show up at team meetings, questioning program priorities. She'd send emails asking for status updates on reports that had been sitting for months. She treated symptoms as emergencies. My team was getting frustrated, and our work suffered.

Here's what happened inside my head: *She doesn't understand our program. She's micromanaging based on outdated metrics. I need to protect my team from her interference. Why can't she see that this is just bureaucratic nonsense that's distracting from actual engineering work?* My defensive internal dialogue corrupted my ability to architect an effective collaboration. When leaders operate from ego protection, they destroy the very emotional infrastructure we need to solve technical problems effectively.

Every technical instinct I had screamed to defend my position. To prove Beck wrong with better data. To demonstrate that their concerns were misplaced and their interference was counterproductive.

I started with logic, thinking I could solve this with facts. I put together charts showing our nonconformance rates compared to system complexity. I explained our risk assessment process. I laid out why these particular issues weren't blocking critical path work.

Logic didn't work.

If anything, my data-driven approach seemed to make Beck more persistent. She kept finding new angles to question our priorities, new reasons we needed to address these issues immediately.

I was so worked up about defending myself to Beck. Then I realized I was fighting my ego. As an Emotional Architect, my internal emotional state becomes part of the infrastructure I'm building. If I'm operating from defensiveness and ego protection, I'm adding dysfunction into every collaboration.

Origin Story:
The Drum and Bugle Corps

My first real lesson about emotional architecture came during my senior year at the Air Force Academy, when I was the Drum Major for the Cadet Drum and Bugle Corps.

I understood the organizational architecture well. As Drum Major, I focused on conducting and performance—the musical work I loved. The Corps Commander handled administrative duties and organizational management. This separation of roles worked beautifully for musical organizations throughout the Air Force.

Then, our director announced a reorganization that would combine both roles into a single position. I would be expected to serve as both Drum Major and Corps Commander.

I knew this was wrong from an organizational perspective. The roles required different skill sets. Combining them would compromise both functions. Every successful musical organization kept these roles separate for good reason.

I prepared my case with perfect technical logic: how the dual role would compromise both functions, why the existing structure served our mission better, and what the best practices were across similar organizations.

I presented my analysis expecting the obvious response: "You're right, let's keep the proven structure." Instead, I got, "The decision is already made. This is how we're moving forward."

I didn't understand how to build the emotional foundation that would allow my technical correctness to be heard and integrated. I had focused entirely on being right while ignoring the human system dynamics that determined whether being right mattered.

I failed to consider what pressures might drive this decision. I hadn't asked what problems the director was trying to solve with this reorganization. I hadn't explored what constraints he might be operating under that weren't obvious to me. I offered no space for him to save face if he wanted to reconsider.

Instead of designing a collaboration where we could solve the underlying problem together, I built a confrontation where someone had to win and someone had to lose.

He held firm on the decision. I was deeply convinced that I was right and he was wrong. So, I drew a line in the sand. "If this is the direction we're going, I can't be part of it." I expected my three years of proven leadership to carry weight. I expected being technically correct to trump organizational politics. I expected the superior logic of my position to prevail. What I had built was a situation where he could either admit he was wrong (publicly undermining his authority) or accept my ultimatum and let me walk away. He chose the latter.

I quit—not just my role as Drum Major, but the entire Corps. I walked away from an organization I'd invested years in building, from relationships with fellow musicians who depended on my leadership, from a major competition that was at the season's beginning.

The timing made my departure even more destructive to the emotional architecture of the group. My exit right before a major competition left the corps scrambling and my fellow musicians feeling abandoned.

I had been technically right and systematically wrong. My technical analysis was flawless. My emotional architecture was catastrophic.

Being right means nothing if you haven't designed the emotional conditions for your rightness to be integrated into solutions that work. The most elegant technical insights become worthless if they're delivered through an emotional infrastructure that makes collaboration impossible.

That experience taught me that as a technical leader, you're responsible for building the emotional systems that allow right answers to emerge and be implemented effectively. Sometimes the most technically sound approach fails not because it's wrong, but because the human system isn't designed to support it.

Years later, I would learn that effective Emotional Architects focus less on being the smartest person in the room and more on creating the conditions where collective intelligence can emerge, even when that means letting go of being personally, individually right.

Architecting a Different Conversation

Once I recognized my ego corrupted the emotional infrastructure of our collaboration, I had to redesign my approach with Beck. Instead of defending my position, I made space for her expertise. The next time she raised concerns about our nonconformance reports, I responded differently. "Beck, I can see these numbers are concerning from a quality perspective. Help me understand what you're seeing that I might be missing."

Shifting from defending my technical analysis to creating space for hers changed everything about our dynamic. Instead of battling over who was right, we were suddenly collaborating to understand a complex problem from multiple angles. Beck wasn't questioning our technical competence. She was operating under pressure from senior managers, who were nervous about program reviews. The nonconformance numbers looked bad on executive dashboards, regardless of their actual technical significance. Her persistence was driven by a desire to help us avoid negative attention from people who didn't understand the technical context.

Once I understood the actual problem she was trying to solve, I could create a solution that worked for both of us. We developed a communication strategy that gave her the status updates she needed for management reporting while protecting my team's time for actual engineering work. We created a system where she could demonstrate quality oversight without disrupting our technical priorities.

I learned that disagreement itself is actually positive. The problem is building collaborations where defensiveness and ego protection make it impossible to find solutions that serve everyone's actual needs.

The most elegant technical solution fails if the human system isn't designed to implement it. The most brilliant individual insight becomes worthless if it can't be integrated into collective action. As an Emotional Architect, you don't win when you're right. Your job is to design conditions where the right answers can emerge and be acted upon effectively.

The Emotional Architect's Ego Problem

Every Emotional Architect faces this challenge when their expertise gets challenged and every instinct screams to prove they're right. We all have egos. They become a problem when we dig in on being technically correct. We've spent years developing expertise, solving complex problems, and earning respect through intellectual competence. When someone questions our technical judgment, it challenges our identity.

Here's the trap: the moment you get defensive, you stop being curious. When you stop being curious, you stop leading.

I could feel it happening in real time during those early conversations with Beck. Every question she asked triggered an internal monologue: *Does she think I don't understand risk assessment? Is she questioning my competence? How can she not see that this is a waste of time? I need to establish that I know what I'm doing here.*

The internal noise was so loud that I couldn't hear what Beck was trying to tell me. I was so busy defending my technical judgment that I completely missed the human concerns driving her persistence.

The Emotional Labor of Staying Curious

The hardest part of managing difficult conversations is the internal emotional work required to stay open when every instinct tells you to close down. When Beck kept pushing on the nonconformance reports, here's what I was managing inside my head:

Threat Response: My nervous system interpreted her challenges as attacks on my competence. Every question felt like evidence she didn't trust my judgment.

Identity Protection: Years of building my reputation on technical excellence made any questioning feel like a threat to my professional identity.

Responsibility Weight: I carried the success of the entire program on my shoulders, and any suggestion that I wasn't managing risks properly felt like a direct challenge to my ability to do my job.

Team Protection Instinct: Watching my engineers get frustrated by what seemed like unnecessary bureaucracy triggered my protective instincts, making me want to fight off the interference.

Authority Anxiety: As a relatively new chief engineer, I feared that backing down or admitting uncertainty would undermine my authority with both my team and my management.

The conversation I needed to have with Beck required me to set aside all that internal chaos and get genuinely curious about her perspective. When I got defensive, I realized I needed to apply the same approach that had worked with my team—asking questions first and judging second.

How This Shows Up Everywhere: The Emotional Architect's Defensiveness

The same defensive patterns that showed up in technical disagreements appeared elsewhere in my life, revealing something uncomfortable about how I approached responsibility and collaboration. When you become the person who makes most of the decisions—what Eric Berne would call the "parent" role in his transactional analysis framework[7] —any input from others can trigger an unexpected defensive response. Even when that input is exactly what you've been asking for.

Berne's framework helps explain why this happens: when we consistently operate in the "parent" ego state, making decisions and managing outcomes for others, we can unconsciously see their input as challenges to our competence rather than contributions to collaborative success.

Here's how this played out in my life at home. "What do you want for dinner?" I asked, scrolling through delivery options on my phone.

---

7   Berne, E. (1964). Games People Play: The Psychology of Human Relationships. Grove Press.

I expected the usual response: *I don't care* or *whatever you want* or *I'm fine with anything*. I'd grown so accustomed to carrying the decision-making burden that I'd begun to prefer it. At least when I chose, someone else's choice couldn't disappoint me.

"How about Italian?" came the response.

Here's what happened in my head in the split second before I responded. *Wait, I had already mentally settled on Thai food. Now I have to reconsider my choice. They're questioning my process. Do they think I can't pick a good restaurant? I've been managing dinner decisions successfully for months—why are they second-guessing me now?*

I was so surprised by someone expressing a preference that my first reaction was irritation rather than relief. Instead of celebrating that someone had engaged with the decision, I heard their suggestion as criticism of my process.

"Well, too bad," I said curtly. "We're not having that tonight."

The silence that followed was immediate and uncomfortable. I'd asked for input and then rejected it dismissively. What followed was a tense evening of hurt feelings, all because I'd conflated someone's engagement with criticism of my authority.

Recognizing the Pattern

This is the same pattern that almost derailed my relationship with Beck. Someone challenges my approach or offers an alternative, my ego interprets their input as competence questioning. I become defensive instead of curious, and I shut down collaboration to protect my authority. The result is that everyone loses: no learning happens, relationships suffer, and better solutions don't emerge.

With dinner, the stakes were low enough that I could see the pattern clearly. With Beck, the stakes felt so high that I couldn't recognize I was doing the same thing.

When you've absorbed responsibility for outcomes, any input from others can feel like criticism rather than collaboration. The more decisions you carry alone, the more defensive you become when others try to share that load.

Understanding the Defensive Triggers

That evening became my early warning system for technical leadership. When I feel that defensive surge in technical discussions, I now recognize it as a signal that my ego is interfering with my judgment. The same defensive triggers I experienced over dinner decisions were operating at a much higher stakes level in our technical disagreements.

My nervous system interpreted challenges as threat responses. I saw technical disagreements as attacks on my competence rather than collaborative problem-solving. Years of building a reputation on technical excellence made any questioning feel personal, creating what I now recognize as identity protection mode. There was also what I came to understand as authority anxiety—the fear that backing down or changing course would undermine my credibility with both the team and leadership. The conversation I needed to have with Beck required me to set aside all that internal noise and get genuinely curious about their perspective. That's much easier said than done when your ego is shouting at you.

Applying Emotional Architecture to Peer Conflicts

When I got defensive with Beck, I remembered something Eric had said during one of our coffee meetings, "You know what I noticed about you, Lisa? You ask questions first and judge second. That's why we trust you." If I could extend that same curiosity to Beck with the same patience I'd learned to show my team, maybe we could find a path forward.

Things shifted when I recognized that the same emotional architecture skills that had transformed my team relationships could transform how I handled technical disagreements with peers. Asking for input while being emotionally unprepared to receive it is worse than not asking at all.

The dinner incident taught me I needed to do internal preparation before engaging in any conversation where I might receive input that challenged my thinking. This meant acknowledging to myself that I might be wrong, that others might see problems I couldn't see, and that changing course based on better information was a sign of leadership strength, not weakness.

Once I understood that my defensive reactions were predictable patterns rather than justified responses to unreasonable behavior, I could start managing them more skillfully. Eliminating my defensive feelings felt like a good approach, but they were actually useful signals that something important was at stake. The goal was to pause long enough between feeling defensive and responding so I could choose curiosity over ego protection.

The Technical Translation: How Dinner Defensiveness Shows Up at Work

The same defensive pattern that made me insufferable over restaurant choices also infiltrated my technical leadership. I didn't recognize it at first because the context felt so different. During team meetings, I'd ask what seemed like an open question, "What do you think about this technical approach?" When someone responded with, "Have we considered approach X instead?" my brain would immediately translate this as an attack on my technical judgment. *Don't they trust my analysis? Why are they questioning me?* Instead of exploring their suggestion, I'd shut it down, "We've already committed to this direction. Let's focus on the implementation."

Stakeholder reviews followed the same pattern. I'd present our recommended solution, feeling confident in the analysis I'd done. When someone brought up "that alternative we discussed last month," my internal alarm bells would start ringing. *I have already done this analysis. Why are they bringing up old options? Do they think I haven't considered everything?* My response would be dismissive, "That approach has significant limitations we've already addressed."

Cross-team collaborations were the worst. I'd spend days developing an integration plan, proud of how I'd worked through all the constraints and requirements. When another team lead mentioned they'd "had success with a different integration pattern," I'd feel that familiar surge of defensiveness. *Are they saying my plan won't work? They don't understand our constraints.* I'd respond with barely concealed irritation, "Our situation is different. This approach won't work for our requirements."

The cycle was maddeningly consistent. I'd develop an approach, someone would offer input or alternatives, I'd interpret their contribution as criticism of my competence, then defend my position instead of exploring their perspective. Whenever collaboration stopped, learning stopped, and better solutions slipped away unexamined.

The technical leadership trap became clear once I could see it: the more expertise you develop, the more your ego becomes invested in your technical judgment. When someone questions your approach, the natural response is to be defensive of your solution. It can feel like they are challenging your identity as a technical expert.

What I eventually learned was that the same emotional work that helps you navigate personal defensiveness—recognizing that ego surge, pausing before responding, choosing curiosity over self-protection—is exactly what technical leadership requires. The skills transfer completely, even when the stakes feel entirely different.

The Power of a Pause

I stopped fighting with Beck and started wondering. Instead of sending another email with more charts, I asked her to meet privately. Not in a conference room with agendas and slides. Just the two of us, away from the performance pressure of an audience.

Before that meeting, I had a conversation with myself. I sat in my office and forced myself to ask: *What if Beck is seeing something I'm missing? What if her persistence comes from genuine concern? What if I'm so focused on being right that I'm missing the point entirely?*

That internal shift from defensive to curious was the hardest part of the entire interaction.

I was nervous as I walked to our meeting. Instead of leading with my technical analysis, I said, "Help me understand what you're seeing that I might be missing. I want to make sure we're addressing the right problem here."

Beck told me about a previous program where mounting nonconformance reports had masked a systemic design issue. By the time they caught it, it was too late to implement fixes for the next vehicle. The program had to absorb significant cost and schedule impacts that could have been avoided if they'd addressed the reports earlier.

Her story surprised me. Not because it was unbelievable, but because she trusted me enough to share her fears and worries. I saw her concerns in a new light. She wasn't being bureaucratic. She was trying to prevent a repeat of a painful experience. Now that I understood her concerns, we started problem-solving together to ensure nothing important fell through the cracks.

The View from Outside: Understanding Beck's Perspective

When I looked at Beck's external pressures, it reframed our communication challenge. Her feedback regarding my program was not driven by malice or an exertion of bureaucratic authority. She was responding to directives from her management and addressing what appeared to be a concerning pattern across multiple programs.

From Beck's perspective, she saw patterns across the organization that concerned her. Our program's nonconformance numbers looked problematic when viewed in isolation, without the context of our system complexity or risk categorization. She had a clear directive from her management: reduce these numbers across all programs, sparing no expense in doing so.

Beck was also fighting her own battles for professional credibility. She needed to prove her value to senior management by demonstrating proactive quality management. When I pushed back on her concerns, it probably felt like I was undermining her credibility with her own management.

Once I understood we were both trying to serve program success, I could approach the conversation as an ally rather than an adversary. We had different perspectives on how to achieve it, and we were each optimizing for different metrics rather than evaluating the entire system.

The solution we eventually developed served both of our needs: a risk-based prioritization system that addressed Beck's concerns about tracking and closure while protecting my team's focus on critical work. Beck could report meaningful progress to her management, and my team could work on high-impact issues without getting buried in administrative tasks that didn't improve our actual performance.

When It Goes Wrong:
The Family Vacation

The same defensive patterns that showed up in technical disagreements appeared in other areas of my life, with more personal consequences than professional ones. I spent months planning what I thought would be the perfect family summer vacation—a Wyoming and South Dakota national parks road trip that would combine fun with learning. I researched routes and ideal driving times, identified historical sites, and created what I believed was the best balance of education and adventure.

When I presented the carefully crafted itinerary to the family, my teenager looked it over and suggested, "Can we add Reptile Gardens?" He pointed to a tourist attraction that was far off our well-planned route.

My immediate internal response was frustration. I'd spent months creating this plan, weighing options, and considering everyone's interests. This random tourist attraction would add hours to our driving time and didn't fit the theme I'd worked so hard to develop.

"That's not what we're going for," I said dismissively. "It's way off our route, and it's not meaningful enough to justify the detour."

The hurt in his expression was immediate. "I thought this was supposed to be a 'family' vacation," he whispered.

What followed was a tense standoff that lasted two days. My teenager felt like his input didn't matter. I felt unappreciated for all the planning work I'd done. My partner was caught in the middle, trying to mediate between my need to be right about the itinerary and our son's desire to contribute something he cared about.

Finally, I forced myself to ask the question I should have started with. "What's so important about Reptile Gardens?"

It turned out he had a genuine interest in reptiles and saw this as an opportunity to learn more about them. While it wasn't the kind of experience I'd envisioned, it represented something he was genuinely curious about. Exactly what I'd been trying to create with the historical sites.

We ended up going. Honestly, it was more fun than I'd imagined. A little cheesy in places, although we all enjoyed the break from my detailed plan. More importantly, including his suggestion transformed the trip from "Mom's educational vacation" into something that felt like a family adventure.

The irony was painful: I'd spent months trying to create the perfect family experience, but I'd almost ruined it by refusing to let the family participate in shaping what that experience looked like.

The Internal Battle of Technical Humility

Staying curious when your expertise is challenged requires a level of emotional maturity that has nothing to do with your technical competence.

You have to be willing to:

Admit you might be wrong without feeling like it undermines your entire professional identity.

Ask questions that reveal your ignorance without fearing that people will lose confidence in your leadership.

Consider perspectives that challenge your analysis without interpreting them as personal attacks.

Change your position based on new information without feeling like you're betraying your previous judgment.

Acknowledge others' expertise without feeling like it diminishes your own value.

Every one of these requires you to set aside the ego protection that got you promoted in the first place.

The technical skills that made me (and you) a successful individual contributor—confidence in my analysis, conviction about my recommendations, persistence in defending my positions—were actively working against me as a leader.

When Your Team Watches You Get Challenged

One of the most difficult aspects of managing your own ego during conflict is that your team is watching how you handle challenges to your authority.

When Beck questioned our priorities in team meetings, I could see my engineers looking to me for protection. They expected me to defend our approach, to push back against what seemed like unnecessary interference, to demonstrate I had the authority to shield them from bureaucratic demands. Part of me wanted to play that role, to be the strong leader who fights off external pressure and protects the team from distraction.

Real strength sometimes looks like vulnerability. Protecting the team meant finding collaborative solutions, not fighting off challenges. The day I told my team, "Beck has raised some valid concerns that I want us to address," I could see the confusion on their faces. Was I backing down? Was I not confident in our approach?

It took time for them to understand that acknowledging valid concerns while maintaining our technical position was stronger leadership than reflexive defensiveness. The shift happened gradually. When Beck's questions led us to catch a potential issue before it became a problem, Eric mentioned that maybe the extra scrutiny wasn't such a bad thing. When our collaborative approach with her sped up the approval process rather than slowing it down, Maria saw the strategic value. When they watched me handle challenges by getting curious rather than defensive, they trusted I could protect the team's interests without having to fight every battle. They realized that strength as a leader meant being confident enough to examine their own assumptions, not defend them.

The Conversation I Had With Myself

You know those conversations you have with yourself in the shower, or while you're on a walk, or late at night when you can't sleep? (No, it's only me?) The conversation with Beck about our nonconformance list showed me that I really needed to understand my own resistance:

Was I fighting for the right technical approach, or was I fighting to avoid admitting I might have overlooked something important?

Was I protecting my team from unnecessary work, or was I protecting my ego from the suggestion that my risk assessment might be incomplete?

Was I standing on principle, or was I being stubborn?

What if Beck was right that we needed to pay more attention to these reports?

What if my dismissal of her concerns was exactly the kind of technical arrogance that leads to serious problems down the road?

This line of questions was brutal because I saw that at least part of my resistance was about ego protection, not technical judgment. I was so invested in being right that I'd stopped being open to the possibility that there might be multiple right answers to this problem.

The Turnaround

Three months later, I was sitting in my office when Beck knocked on my door. "Got a minute?" she asked. "I want to run something by you before it becomes an issue." This time, instead of a formal presentation about compliance failures, Beck came to me early with a pattern they'd noticed in supplier quality reports. She brought this as a collaborative heads-up. There was no accusation. "I'm seeing some trends that remind me of that other program I mentioned," Beck said, spreading out the data. "Nothing urgent yet. I thought we should get ahead of it."

That conversation led to a proactive quality improvement initiative that prevented what could have been a significant problem six months later. More importantly, it demonstrated that our difficult conversation had strengthened our working relationship.

What struck me was how naturally we worked together to address the problem. Instead of the adversarial dynamic that had characterized our early interactions, we'd developed a collaborative relationship built on mutual respect for each other's expertise and concerns.

The transformation was as much professional as it was personal. Beck later told me that our original conflict had taught her something important about how to raise concerns without triggering defensiveness. "I learned to lead with curiosity instead of conclusions," she said. "When I understand what you're trying to protect, I can figure out how to help you protect it while also addressing my concerns."

For my part, Beck became one of my most trusted advisors precisely because I knew she would tell me hard truths in ways that strengthened rather than damaged our working relationship. When she brought me concerns, I knew they were based on genuine technical merit rather than organizational politics or a personal agenda.

The Long-Term Impact

The conflict with Beck changed my approach to subsequent stakeholder disagreements. Instead of starting with my technical analysis and trying to convince others I was right, I learned to start with curiosity about what they were trying to accomplish.

The framework we developed—understanding underlying concerns before addressing surface positions—became my standard approach for navigating technical conflicts. When other programs asked me to help resolve similar disagreements, I taught the same lesson Beck had inadvertently taught me: most technical conflicts are trust and communication that look like technical ones.

Three years later, when we were celebrating a successful launch, Beck was one of the first people to congratulate me.

"You've learned to fight for the mission instead of fighting to be right," she said. "That's what makes someone ready for senior leadership."

Beck had become one of my most valuable early warning systems. She now trusts me to listen to her concerns without getting defensive. That makes her focus on being thorough even more valuable. The message stuck with me: when you can navigate conflict with curiosity instead of defensiveness; you shift out of problem-solving and build the relationships that prevent future problems.

After learning to navigate my ego battles (or at least being aware that I have them), I could recognize when others were trapped in the same defensive patterns. The most effective way I've found to help people escape the ego trap is to ask questions that shift their focus from being right to getting results. When I see someone getting defensive about their approach, I've learned to pause the technical discussion and get curious about their underlying goals. What I've discovered aligns with Julian Rotter's[8] groundbreaking research on locus of control from the 1960s. He found that people who believe they can influence outcomes through their own actions handle conflict differently than those who feel like things just happen to them.

Rotter's research revealed that individuals operate from either an internal locus of control (believing their actions directly influence outcomes) or an external locus of control (believing outcomes are determined by external forces, luck, or other people's decisions). This distinction turns out to be crucial for

---

8   Rotter, J. B. (1966). Generalized expectancies for internal versus external control of reinforcement. *Psychological Monographs: General and Applied*, 80(1), 1-28.

understanding why some technical professionals get stuck in defensive patterns while others remain collaborative even during disagreements.

People with an internal locus of control approach technical conflicts as problems to be solved. When someone challenges their approach, they think, "What can I learn from this perspective? How might I adjust my solution to address their concerns? What would I need to do differently to get the outcome we all want?" They stay focused on what they can control and influence.

People with an external locus of control approach the same conflicts as battles to be won or lost. This shows up frequently in technical environments. I've found that when engineers get defensive about their technical approaches, it's often because they feel like their competence is being questioned rather than their solution being refined. The external locus of control makes them feel like they need to defend their entire professional identity rather than discussing one technical decision.

The key insight from Rotter's research is that you can help people shift their locus of control by changing the questions you ask. Instead of arguing about whose technical approach is better, you can redirect their attention to what they can control and influence.

The most productive team members—the ones who rarely get trapped in defensive patterns—are the ones who maintain an internal locus of control. They focus on what they can control and to shape outcomes rather than react to them. They ask questions like, "What would I need to learn to make this work?" "How could I modify my approach to address these concerns?" "What can I do to move us toward the best possible outcome?"

When I help someone shift from "I need to prove I'm right" to "I need to figure out how to make this work," the ego battle usually dissolves on its own. They stop defending their positions and start problem-solving toward their actual goals.

When coaching others through these situations, I use a framework of outcome-focused questions:

"What does success look like for this project/program/ mission?" This question shifts focus from being right to being effective. Often, people realize their ego investment is working against the outcomes they care about.

"What would you do if you had to make this work with (the other person's) input?" This forces creative problem-solving rather than positional defending. It acknowledges their expertise while requiring them to integrate other perspectives.

"How might your future self look back on this situation?" This creates emotional distance that helps people see beyond their immediate defensive responses.

"What are you protecting, and is it worth protecting at this cost?" Sometimes the thing we're protecting (our reputation for being right) is less important than what we're sacrificing (relationships, outcomes, learning opportunities).

Learning to Manage My Own Defensiveness

The hardest part of that conversation with Beck was managing the voice in my head that was screaming, *She doesn't understand our program! She's micromanaging! I need to prove her wrong!*

After years of catching myself getting defensive in important conversations and then having to repair the damage afterward, I realized I needed to get better at managing my own internal chaos. The same systematic approach I used for technical problems needed to apply to the moments when my ego got hijacked.

I learned you can't engineer your way out of defensive reactions by being smarter or more prepared. When someone challenges your technical judgment, your nervous system doesn't care how well you know the specifications. It knows something feels threatening and activates every fight-or-flight response you have.

It's normal to feel triggered when someone questions your competence. I'd never learned what to do with that surge of defensive energy besides either suppressing it (which never worked) or letting it drive my response (which always made things worse).

What I needed was a way to catch myself in the moment, before I said something that would turn a technical disagreement into a relationship problem. Through a lot of trial and (mostly) error, I figured out an approach that worked when the pressure was on:

First, I had to learn to notice when my body was moving into defend-mode. My shoulders would tense up. Heat would creep up my neck. My heart would start racing even though we were having a conversation. I'd catch myself mentally preparing counterarguments while the other person was still talking, which meant I wasn't listening anymore.

These were my early warning signals that my nervous system was treating a technical discussion like a personal attack.

Once I could recognize the pattern, I learned to create a pause. Sometimes taking a slow, deep breath was enough to interrupt the defensive spiral. Other times I'd ask myself,

What am I protecting right now? My reputation? My authority? My sense of being right?

I reminded myself that curiosity would serve the mission better than defensiveness. There's this technique where you give your triggered inner voice a name—I called mine "Jonathan"—and when I'd feel him taking over, I'd think, *Not now, Jonathan. Let me listen first.* (My apologies to anyone named Jonathan or who loves one. It's not about you.)

The hardest part was learning to reframe what was happening. Instead of assuming they were questioning my competence, I practiced thinking, *They're bringing a different perspective that I might not have considered. Instead of, They don't understand our constraints, I'd try, I might not be explaining our constraints clearly enough.*

It sounds simple, but when your ego is activated, simple isn't easy.

Finally, I learned to get genuinely curious. Instead of building my defense, I'd ask questions: "What are you seeing that I might be missing?" "Help me understand what's driving your concern." "What would need to be true for this approach to work from your perspective?"

The Beck conversation was one of the first times I used this approach successfully. Instead of defending our nonconformance management with better data, I got curious about her experience and discovered concerns I never would have uncovered by being right.

While this approach doesn't eliminate the discomfort of being challenged, it keeps that discomfort from hijacking conversations that could solve problems.

The Long-Term Cost of Technical Ego

When technical leaders consistently choose ego protection over curiosity, the costs compound over time in ways that slowly strangle the very technical excellence they're trying to protect.

The first thing that happens is that people stop giving you honest feedback. They learn that challenging your position triggers defensiveness, so they find safer ways to communicate, or they stop communicating altogether. Your blind spots multiply because the people closest to the work know that pointing out problems creates more problems.

Innovation stagnates as team members stop bringing creative ideas that might question established approaches. Why suggest a better way of doing something when you know it will be interpreted as a criticism of the current way? The technical solutions that could make your systems more elegant, more efficient, or more maintainable never reach your attention.

Relationships with stakeholders and other teams deteriorate as people learn that engaging directly with you is too difficult. They work around you rather than with you, excluding you from conversations where your technical input would be valuable. You become isolated precisely when you need collaboration most.

Problems that could have been addressed early grow into major crises because people stopped raising concerns. The small issues your team noticed months ago—the ones they decided weren't worth the fight—compounded into the big problems that blindside you during critical moments.

Perhaps most damaging of all, emerging leaders on your team never learn to navigate complex stakeholder dynamics because they only see defensive responses to challenges. They don't develop the skills to welcome disagreement, integrate different perspectives, or find collaborative solutions because they've never seen those skills modeled.

A technical leader who can't manage their ego becomes a bottleneck that constrains everything else. Their expertise, which should be an asset that elevates the entire team, becomes a liability that limits what the team can accomplish together.

Reflection Framework: Managing Your Internal War

The biggest challenge in navigating disagreement isn't managing the other person; it's managing your own ego when you feel challenged or misunderstood.

Consider Your Recent Disagreements

What topics or challenges consistently make you feel defensive? Notice the patterns. Do you struggle when you feel your technical expertise is questioned? Do you get frustrated when someone suggests a different approach? When you feel that defensiveness rising, what's actually being challenged—your technical judgment or your position in the hierarchy?

In your last few disagreements, did you ask more questions or make more statements? When someone challenges your thinking, do you get curious about their perspective, or do you build your counterargument while they're still talking?

What are you protecting when you get defensive? Sometimes it's your reputation, sometimes it's your identity as the technical expert, sometimes it's fear that admitting uncertainty will undermine your authority.

How often do you change your position based on new information versus sticking to your initial assessment? The ability to evolve your thinking is often what separates effective technical leaders from technically competent people who can't lead.

One Thing to Try This Week

The next time someone challenges your technical approach, pause before responding and ask yourself, "What am I protecting right now?" Then try responding with genuine curiosity, "What are you seeing that I might be missing?" Notice how both the conversation and your internal state shift when you choose curiosity over defensiveness.

Playbook:
Designing Collaboration
When Smart People Disagree

The goal is to architect emotional infrastructure that enables disagreement to generate better solutions rather than defensive battles.

When You Feel Defensive in Technical Discussions

When disagreements happen, it's easy to prepare counterarguments instead of trying to understand the other person's perspective.

Watch for ego protection disguised as technical rigor, rushing to defend before you understand the real issue, or treating disagreement as a threat rather than valuable information.

Recognize the infrastructure risk: "My defensiveness is damaging the emotional foundation we need for collaboration."

Pause and redesign: "What would I need to feel safe enough to be wrong here? What does the other person need to feel heard?"

Create space for their expertise: "Help me understand what you're seeing that I might be missing."

Architect joint problem-solving: "What problem are we both trying to solve here? How can we design a solution that addresses both our concerns?"

The most valuable action you can take here is becoming aware of your defensiveness. Instead of letting the feeling of being challenged drive the discussion, look for ways that you can collaborate. This is easier said than done, but once you can recognize defensiveness, it gets easier to find common ground, and that will also soften the team's approach to disagreement. Seeing their leader reach for collaboration will encourage the team to do so as well.

When Someone Challenges Your Technical Decisions

This is a little different from the earlier situation. Here, you are being challenged after a decision has already been made. Your immediate impulse is to prove you're right rather than explore whether you might be incomplete.

Watch out for making disagreement personal, treating questions as attacks on your competence, or creating win/lose dynamics when collaboration is possible.

Design curiosity into your response: "That's an interesting point. Walk me through your thinking on this."

Create shared ownership: "What would need to be true for both our approaches to make sense? Are we solving different parts of the same problem?"

Separate technical merit from personal validation: "Let's focus on what approach best serves the mission, regardless of who came up with it."

Create space for face-saving solutions: "How can we integrate the best parts of both approaches?"

The same awareness of your defensiveness applies here. You may have to change your decision or add additional rationale. This can be more difficult if your management chain is already invested in a decision. Sometimes, you'll find your original decision was the right one, and you'll have to deal with the team feeling like they weren't fully invested. Check in with the "difficult topics" playbook in chapter 2.

When You Need to Challenge Someone Else's Technical Approach

Challenging your team can be something that you find easy, or it might be something you avoid because you're concerned about their solution and want to raise questions without creating defensiveness.

Watch out for making them wrong to make yourself right, questioning their competence instead of exploring their reasoning, or creating public challenges that force defensive responses.

Build safety first. "I want to make sure I understand your approach fully before raising any concerns."

Frame challenges as collaboration: "I'm seeing some potential issues—can we explore these together?"

Design space for them to maintain dignity: "Your solution addresses X well. I'm wondering about Y—how were you thinking about that?"

Build on their expertise: "Given your experience with Z, what do you think about this consideration?"

Challenging someone else's approach isn't a personal attack. Some people have a life experience that makes them uncomfortable with challenging others because of strong negative reactions from the person being challenged. Leading with curiosity and asking questions is a great way to learn more and offer your experience without creating instant defensiveness.

When the Team Is Divided on Technical Approaches

Sometimes challenging problems can cause multiple people to have valid technical perspectives. This disagreement might create faction dynamics.

Watch out for letting disagreement become identity-based, allowing expertise hierarchies to shut down good ideas, or rushing to decisions without achieving genuine consensus.

Architect shared problem-solving: "It sounds like we have multiple good approaches to different aspects of this challenge. How do we design a solution that captures the best insights from everyone?"

Create a neutral space: "Let's step back from advocating for solutions and focus on understanding the full scope of what we're trying to solve."

Design collaborative evaluation: "What criteria should we use to evaluate these approaches? How do we make sure we're considering all the important factors?"

Build shared ownership: "How can we create a solution that everyone can support, even if it's not exactly what they initially proposed?"

When you move the team from competing positions to shared problem-solving, technical disagreements become opportunities for better solutions. Technical excellence requires rigorous evaluation of competing ideas—the challenge is preventing debate from fracturing the team's capacity to work together. Teams that can disagree productively on technical approaches while maintaining trust deliver stronger solutions than teams where everyone agrees too quickly.

When Disagreement Is Stalling Progress

Disagreement can keep your team from solving problems. When your team is stuck in analysis paralysis or circular debates about technical approaches, it's tough to redirect.

Watch out for using disagreement to avoid the risk of decision-making, perfectionism that prevents progress, or letting the fear of being wrong stop forward movement.

Recognize the failure: "We have good technical thinking, but haven't designed a way to integrate it into decisions."

Design decision-making structure: "What information do we need to move forward? Who needs to be involved in this decision?"

Set time boundaries: "Let's spend 30 minutes exploring this fully, then commit to a path forward we can all support."

Create a learning infrastructure: "How will we know if our chosen approach is working? What will we do if we need to adjust?"

This kind of being stuck is often a great opportunity to do a retrospective where each person explores what kept them from being able to get aligned with the proposed solution.

The Ongoing Practice

Managing your ego during difficult conversations isn't a skill you master once. It's a practice you maintain throughout your entire leadership journey. Even now, years later, I still feel that familiar surge of defensiveness when someone questions my technical judgment. I've learned to recognize it quickly and choose curiosity over ego protection.

I'm not always successful. I still have conversations where I realize afterward that I spent more energy defending my position than understanding theirs. I recover faster now, and I'm more willing to circle back and try again. The goal is to manage your ego skillfully so that it serves your leadership rather than constraining it.

In the next chapter, we'll explore how this internal emotional work enables one of the most challenging aspects of technical leadership: navigating the political complexities that surround every technical decision and learning to find solutions that serve both technical excellence and organizational reality.

The Art of Technical Compromise: When Perfect Is the Enemy of Progress

Chapter 5

The data were unambiguous. Sitting in the conference room, looking at the test results spread across the table, the technical path forward couldn't have been clearer. The analysis showed exactly what needed to be done. The physics didn't lie. The math was beautiful in its precision. However, implementing it would add enough cost and schedule to kill the program.

This is the moment that reveals whether you're a technical expert or an Emotional Architect: when you must design human systems that can embrace imperfection in service of mission success. The technical analysis is often clear. The challenge is building team understanding and commitment around solutions that feel technically suboptimal. Anyone can identify the perfect solution. An Emotional Architect creates the conditions where teams can psychologically navigate the gap between what they want to build and what they need to build.

It would be so much easier if technical leadership were about being technically pure. That's not the job. The job is delivering technical excellence within the constraints of the real world—even when the real world doesn't care about your elegant solution.

As a chief engineer, I can insist on the "most technically correct" answer to every decision. I also know that if I do that consistently, we'll get mired in analysis paralysis and the program will get cancelled.

The art of technical leadership isn't choosing between right and wrong. It's choosing between multiple versions of right enough, each with different technical and programmatic trade-offs.

Origin Story:
Better Is the Enemy of Good Enough

Early in my time on Orion, I worked as an operations engineer, and I could see exactly what we needed to do the job right. We were understaffed, overworked, and making the kind of mistakes that come from pushing people beyond their limits.

The solution was obvious to me: hire two additional operations engineers, one electrical and one mechanical. With the right team size, we could have peers for procedure and engineering reviews, catching errors before they became costly rework. We could work opposing shifts so people could take time off without shutting down critical work. We'd be fresher, more clear-headed, and more effective.

I presented my case to the program director with all the confidence of someone who'd done the analysis. "We'd avoid errors in procedures that cost us time and rework," I explained. "We'd finish sooner because the work wouldn't shut down when someone needed a break. We'd be operating at full capacity instead of pushing ourselves to the limits."

He listened patiently to my perfectly logical argument, then delivered a line that would reshape how I thought about engineering excellence, "Lisa, better is the enemy of good enough."

I was frustrated. Here I was, proposing a solution that would improve quality, reduce risk, and increase efficiency, and he told me to settle for less. I'd built my career on exceptional technical performance, and it felt like he was asking me to compromise my standards to fit into his narrow budget constraints.

"We're already running behind and have overspent our budget with months of work still ahead of us," he continued. "The solution isn't to add more people. It's to make do with what we have. Work as much as you can, and don't mess up. Look at what you're doing and see what you can cut."

It felt like professional heresy. I'd been trained to find the best solution, to never settle for adequate when superior was possible. The idea that "good enough" could be the right answer challenged everything I thought I knew about engineering excellence.

I was in for a big surprise when I learned why we'd taken over this work in the first place. The original subcontractor had pursued exactly the approach I advocated. They'd built a larger team, scheduled people with proper time off, and created what looked like a more sustainable operation. They'd spent their entire budget in three months and had their contract cancelled.

We succeeded with the scrappy approach. The flight was a success, even though we were wiped out afterward and took months to recover and get back to full capacity. We learned there was a lot of overhead work that could be cut out, and some tasks that could be handed off to other groups. The "good enough" solution worked within the constraints we were given, while the "better" solution had killed the program entirely.

That program director taught me that technical leadership requires optimizing for mission success *and* seeking technical perfection. Sometimes the greatest technical achievement is delivering a solution that works within the constraints you're given, even when you know a better solution exists.

The Technical Perfectionist's Trap

Engineers are trained to solve problems. We'll test it, analyze it, model it, and prove it. We'll stay late to get the math exactly right. We'll fight for technical integrity because that's what separates good engineering from dangerous shortcuts. This training serves us well as individual contributors. It can destroy us as leaders.

Leadership decisions don't exist in the clean world of optimization problems. They exist at the messy intersection of technical requirements that may conflict with each other, budget constraints that limit what's possible, and schedule pressures that compress decision timelines. You're also dealing with team capabilities that may not match the theoretical ideal, organizational politics that shape what solutions are acceptable, and risk tolerance that varies across stakeholders. Add to this the future uncertainties that make perfect analysis impossible, and you have a decision environment that bears no resemblance to the controlled problems we learned to solve as engineers.

When you insist on technical perfection in this environment, you don't get better engineering. You get paralysis.

The False Choice Between Excellence and Pragmatism

The real choice is between technical perfectionism and technical pragmatism. Between optimizing for theoretical excellence and optimizing for mission success.

Technical perfectionism says: "We will find the best possible solution, regardless of constraints." As any engineer knows, there is always something better.

Technical pragmatism says: "We will find the best solution that can be implemented successfully within our constraints."

The first approach protects your reputation as a brilliant engineer. The second approach protects the mission.

Technical pragmatism, done skillfully, often leads to better long-term outcomes than technical perfectionism. Until it doesn't. There is a limit. When your system becomes a collection of compromises, you're headed toward a reboot. That is a different problem, and perhaps a story for another book.

A suboptimal solution that gets implemented creates learning, generates data, and enables the next iteration of improvement. A perfect solution that never gets built teaches no one anything.

The Chief Engineer's Emotional Burden

What the technical leadership books don't tell you is how these decisions feel when you're making them. Every time you choose the pragmatic path over the optimal path, part of you dies a little. You can see an elegant solution that would work better. You understand the physics more deeply than anyone else in the room. You know exactly how to build something beautiful and you choose the ugly solution that works anyway.

The weight of those choices accumulates over time. Decision after decision where you hold your nose and choose good enough over better. Where you disappoint the brilliant engineers on your team who wanted to solve the problem the right way.

There were nights I went home questioning whether I had become the leader who settles for mediocrity. Whether I betrayed everything I'd been trained to value as an engineer.

On my drive home one day, I thought about this problem and I took the perfectionism/pragmatism concepts from above and reframed what technical excellence means in a leadership context.

Individual contributor excellence: building the most technically elegant solution possible.

Technical leadership excellence: building the most technically effective solution possible within real-world constraints.

The second definition doesn't abandon technical rigor. It applies technical thinking to a more complex problem that includes human and organizational variables alongside the physics.

The Artemis Trade-off: When Perfect is the Enemy of the Mission

There is a specific kind of "technical ego" that thrives in high-stakes environments like NASA. We want the most elegant solution. We want the most advanced sensor. We want the perfect architecture.

During the development of the life support systems for Artemis II, we had a test failure that ground our progress to a halt and sparked an immediate, bitter deadlock. One group of specialists was insisting on a repair and replacement that, on paper, was technically superior. It was cleaner and more efficient. The group responsible for the integration and schedule were terrified. They knew that the elegant solution introduced dozens of unknown variables and risks we couldn't test in time for the launch window. Their preference was to make a workaround for the failed system that allowed us to operate despite the failure. As Chief Engineer, I felt the technical answer was a toss-up. Both sides had data. The emotional answer was where the real work lived.

I spent a month living in the messy middle of these two groups. What I observed wasn't a technical debate; it was a collision of values. For the specialists, backing down felt like a betrayal of their craft—if they weren't building the best possible hardware, what were they even doing? Meanwhile, the integration team was looking at the calendar like it was a ticking clock, terrified that a 'clean' solution today would mean a catastrophic delay tomorrow.

I had to architect a conversation that moved us away from *which part is better?* to *which system allows the mission to succeed?*

We eventually went with the workaround solution. It wasn't the choice that would win an engineering award for innovation (although it did require a lot of creativity), but it was the choice that maximized the mission's integrity and met our demanding schedule. I had to carry the emotional weight of the purists who felt let down, helping them see that their rigor wasn't being rejected—it was being redirected toward the much harder task of integration.

In human spaceflight, pragmatism is an act of love for the crew. It's the incredibly difficult emotional work of swallowing your pride and abandoning your 'perfect' blueprint so that the four people sitting on top of that rocket actually come home. The true labor of the Emotional Architect is holding that tension until the competing egos finally fuse into a shared mission.

How This Shows Up Everywhere: The Balance Between Perfect and Possible

As a technical leader, you'll experience this battle almost every day. Customers want the most perfect solution, and your company wants to deliver something that meets their needs while maintaining profitability. Finding that balance where both sides feel they've gotten a good deal requires understanding what "good enough" means.

My introduction to this concept happened when I worked with a team to build automated orbital maneuver planning software. The goal was straightforward: reduce the time needed to plan maneuvers, reduce errors, and allow planning with fewer reviewers. We delivered software that did exactly that. It was, however, built in Excel, which in 1994 was pretty clunky.

The demo should have been a celebration. We'd met every requirement. Instead, I got an earful about user experience issues I'd never considered. The software worked perfectly from a technical standpoint, but it felt awkward and inefficient to the people who had to use it every day.

That's when I learned to ask different questions: How do you envision interacting with this system? What does your typical workflow look like? What would make this feel intuitive rather than burdensome? Agreement that a program will meet requirements is table stakes. A complete understanding includes how users interact with the system, what process they follow, and how it reduces errors in their daily work. These details are rarely incorporated into requirements yet they significantly influence whether a solution succeeds.

The same tension between perfect and pragmatic shows up everywhere in life. Remember the family vacation planning disaster from the last chapter? I'd spent months optimizing every detail of our National Parks road trip, but my rigid, perfect plan almost prevented us from including my teenager's suggestion for Reptile Gardens, which turned out to be one of the trip's highlights.

In home improvement projects, I've learned that waiting for the perfect solution often means living with broken systems indefinitely. My irrigation system doesn't quite reach all the areas and floods others. I've learned to manage the timer and supplement with hand watering rather than waiting for the budget and time to redesign the entire system. Sometimes, the "good enough" fix that can be implemented immediately is better than the perfect renovation that might happen someday.

The pattern even shows up in relationships and personal growth. You can spend so much time seeking the perfect partner who meets every criterion that you miss building something meaningful with someone who's good enough in the ways that matter most while being exceptional in ways you hadn't anticipated. The key is ensuring your partner meets your minimum needs. When relationships become one-sided, they're set up for resentment and distance down the road.

The same applies to personal development. You can focus so intensely on wanting to do all the right things perfectly that you end up not doing anything at all. Sometimes the most growth comes from being imperfect, making mistakes, and getting better through action rather than waiting until you're ready to be perfect.

The pattern is universal: perfectionism often prevents progress toward better outcomes.

Reading the Full Decision Landscape

My orbital maneuver planning experience—and countless similar situations since—taught me that making pragmatic technical decisions requires reading multiple systems simultaneously. It's not enough to solve the technical problem in isolation. You must understand how your solution fits into a complex web of constraints and consequences.

When I'm facing a decision between the technically perfect solution and the pragmatically viable one, I've learned to systematically examine what I call the full decision landscape. This means asking questions across four critical dimensions:

1. The Technical Reality

The starting point is always the physics and the engineering fundamentals. What does the technical system require? Where are the hard constraints that cannot be negotiated versus the preferences that might be flexible? What are the real risks that could cause mission failure versus the theoretical concerns that feel important and may not be? Which technical paths are genuinely unacceptable from a safety or performance standpoint, and which ones feel uncomfortable because they're different from what we've done before?

I've learned to challenge my own assumptions here: What assumptions are we making that could be questioned? Are we solving the actual problem, or are we solving the problem we're comfortable tackling? Sometimes the most elegant technical solution emerges when you step back and ask whether you're even working on the right challenge.

2. The Human Reality

Technical solutions don't implement themselves; people do. What can your team deliver with its current capabilities and constraints? What timeline pressures are creating urgency that might make a 90% solution delivered on time more valuable than a 100% solution delivered late? What organizational constraints are truly non-negotiable versus the ones that feel fixed and could be influenced?

Who must live with the consequences of this decision? The people who will operate, maintain, and troubleshoot your solution have insights that can make or break its success. What emotional investment do different stakeholders bring to various approaches? Sometimes technical resistance is about the technology. More often, it's about feeling heard and valued in the decision-making process.

3. The Hidden Options

This is where creative problem-solving happens. What alternatives aren't being considered because they don't fit into the obvious categories? Where might we be trapped by false either/or thinking when there are multiple viable paths? What creative approaches could satisfy multiple constraints simultaneously rather than optimizing for one?

I've found that some of the best solutions emerge when you ask: What would we do if all the current options were off the table? How might we reframe the problem to expand the solution space? Which requirements that seem fixed could be reexamined if we were willing to think differently about the challenge?

4. The Long-Term Implications

Finally, every technical decision sets a precedent. What doors does this choice open or close for future programs? How does this decision affect your team's capability development—are you building skills and confidence, or are you creating dependencies and limitations? What organizational learning happens or doesn't happen based on the path you choose?

How does this decision affect stakeholder trust and confidence? A technically imperfect solution that delivers on its promises builds more credibility than a technically elegant solution that fails to account for real-world constraints.

Ultimately, navigating this landscape requires a fundamental shift in how we view our role as technical leaders. It means letting go of the fiction that engineering decisions can be made in a vacuum, isolated from the humans who design, build, and operate the hardware.

When you intentionally map the technical and human realities alongside the hidden options and long-term implications, you stop reacting to crises and start leading with intention. The art of technical compromise never means settling for less or watering down your standards. Successful compromise is optimizing for the right combination of technical excellence and practical success, ensuring that both your systems and your people are built to go the distance.

The Pain of the Practical Compromise

I remember one particularly painful decision where we had to choose between three design approaches for a critical component:

Option A: The Technically Elegant Solution

Beautiful engineering, optimal performance, minimal risk from a physics standpoint. It represented everything I'd been trained to value as an engineer. The thermal management was exquisite. The structural efficiency was remarkable. The interface design was clean and extensible.

The problem was this approach would push us past our launch window, blow through our remaining budget reserves, and require expertise that would take months to develop or acquire. It was the kind of solution that looked perfect on paper. It almost completely ignored what we could execute.

Option B: The Heritage Approach

Proven technology, well understood, minimal development risk. I could point to three previous programs where similar designs had worked flawlessly. The team knew how to build it. The suppliers knew how to deliver it.

It was heavier than our mass budget allowed and would require significant modifications to other subsystems. More importantly, it represented no advancement in our technical capabilities. We'd be building the same thing we built five years ago.

Option C: The "Good Enough" Compromise

Not technically optimal but achievable with our current team within our schedule constraints. It borrowed proven elements from heritage designs while incorporating targeted improvements that our team could realistically implement.

It would work, but every engineer in the room could see ways it could be better. The thermal design was adequate but not elegant. The structural approach was heavier than optimal but lighter than heritage. The interfaces were functional but not beautiful.

Standing in that room, I could feel the weight of everyone's expectations. The engineers wanted me to champion technical excellence. Program management needed a path that wouldn't blow up the schedule. The customer counted on us to deliver capability, and I read that as perfection. The desire to deliver Option A weighed heavily as I wanted to meet the unspoken desire for perfection.

The technically correct choice was Option A. The programmatically viable choice was Option C.

I chose Option C. It felt like swallowing sand. As I held my nose and chose the "good enough" solution, I thought about Eric and that first project. He'd taught me that sometimes the most elegant engineering solution is the one that gets built and teaches you something. Perfect designs in isolation teach no one anything.

I also knew that Option A, for all its technical beauty, could have led to a cancelled program when we missed our delivery window. Option C would get hardware into testing, generate real data, and move the mission forward.

Sometimes leadership means choosing the ugly solution that works over the beautiful solution that doesn't. It requires redefining what "excellence" truly means in a real-world environment. It is easy for an engineer to fall in love with the elegance of a theoretical model, but a leader's responsibility is to the mission as a whole. The most elegant design in the world is useless if it sits on the drawing board while the opportunity to fly passes you by.

Designing Conversations That Enable Compromise

The technical decision was only half the challenge. The other half was building team understanding and buy-in for a solution that none of us loved but all of us could support.

I learned you can't just announce a compromise decision and expect people to embrace it emotionally. You must design the emotional infrastructure that allows people to process the gap between their technical ideals and practical reality without losing their sense of professional integrity.

This meant creating space for people to voice their concerns about 'settling for less.' It meant helping them reframe technical compromise not as failure, but as optimization for different variables. It meant having conversations that preserved their identity as excellent engineers while expanding their definition of what technical excellence meant in a leadership context.

The View from Outside: What Others Were Thinking

The team was disappointed, and I could see it in their faces during the design reviews that followed. They were building something they knew could be better, and I was the person who had decided not to make it better.

Program management felt relieved that we had a path forward that didn't blow up the schedule. They were also nervous about choosing what seemed like the least impressive option. The customer focused on delivering capability on time, knowing their own stakeholders would question why we hadn't chosen the most advanced approach. My management watched to see if I could make tough decisions under pressure or if I would get paralyzed trying to make the best of everything.

One engineer came to my office a few weeks later. "I understand the constraints we're working with, and I want to make sure we're not giving up on technical excellence because it's difficult." That conversation hit me harder than any stakeholder criticism ever could. They were asking the question I asked myself: Had

I become the kind of leader who settles for good enough? The answer, I realized, was more complex than yes or no.

I had become a leader who understands that technical excellence exists within a larger context of mission success. Sometimes, the most technically excellent decision is to choose a suboptimal technical approach that enables the larger mission to succeed. My understanding came at a cost: the constant emotional labor of holding the tension between what could be perfect and what would work.

Why Honesty About Trade-offs Built Trust

When I explained my reasoning openly, "Here's why we're choosing this approach, here's what we're giving up, and here's how we'll manage the downsides"—something unexpected happened. Instead of losing credibility for admitting compromises, I gained trust for being transparent about the decision process.

Teams and stakeholders could accept imperfect solutions when they understood the constraints and trusted that their concerns had been considered. Honesty about limitations turned out to be more valuable than false confidence about perfect solutions.

When Perfect Really Is Required

This doesn't mean that every decision should compromise technical excellence for convenience. Some systems have no tolerance for "good enough":

- Life support systems where failure means death
- Nuclear reactor controls where errors have catastrophic consequences
- Aircraft flight controls where a malfunction causes crashes

- Medical devices where reliability directly affects patient outcomes

Part of technical leadership is knowing when you're operating in a zero-tolerance environment versus when pragmatic trade-offs are appropriate. Even in high-stakes environments, the principles remain the same: understand all your constraints, expand your options, and choose the solution that best serves the mission within the real-world context you're operating in.

On our program, crew safety was rarely negotiable. Within the bounds of safety requirements, we had flexibility to prioritize other factors like cost, schedule, and technical advancement. The key was being explicit about which requirements were absolute constraints and which were optimization targets.

Building Confidence in Imperfect Decisions

Over time, I developed an approach to making technical compromises that I could live with. I didn't make this change because the decisions themselves were flawless, but because I had a systematic way of evaluating trade-offs and ensuring my choices served the mission.

The Budget Meeting That Taught Me About Requirements

Any tech leader knows that budgets drive technical decisions more often than we'd like. One day, in a budget review where we were $2 million over target, the program manager went through our requirements line by line. He asked a simple question about each one, "Is this required for mission success, or is this something we'd like to have?" I watched our "requirements" list shrink dramatically in two hours.

The GPS receiver that could track twelve satellites instead of eight? Nice to have. The backup communication system with triple redundancy? Required. The advanced data processing that cut analysis time in half? Nice to have, but creates future sustainability. The thermal protection that ensured survival in worst-case conditions? Required.

This forced me to distinguish between genuine mission requirements and engineering preferences disguised as requirements. Most of our budget problems came from optimizing for theoretical ideals rather than actual mission needs.

Technical Boundaries

Soon after, I found myself stuck between two equally viable approaches for a critical subsystem. Both met our requirements. Both had solid technical merit. I spent weeks analyzing performance trade-offs without making progress.

Finally, my manager asked me two questions that cut through the analysis paralysis, "What's the worst performance you can accept and still meet the mission?" and "What's the best performance you could achieve if budget and schedule weren't factors?"

As I sat with those questions, I realized I had made an artificial duality between right and wrong. I was really choosing where to operate within a range of acceptable solutions. Mission requirements and physics set the lower boundary. Theoretical possibilities set the upper boundary. Once I understood those boundaries, the decision became about optimizing within constraints rather than pursuing perfection.

When Different Risks Meant Different Strategies

Another decision I faced involved choosing between three approaches that each carried different types of uncertainties. One approach had proven technology but aggressive schedule demands. Another had an innovative design but development unknowns. The third balanced both but required capabilities our team hadn't demonstrated.

I realized I was trying to minimize "risk" as if it were a single number on a spreadsheet, when in reality, each approach required managing completely different challenges:

- The proven technology approach meant managing schedule pressure and potential team burnout.
- The innovative design approach meant managing technical uncertainty and potential performance shortfalls.
- The balanced approach meant managing skill development and learning curves.

Looking at decisions through these different risk profiles helped me choose based on which challenges we were best equipped to handle, rather than trying to find a solution with no risks at all. By reframing the problem this way, I could assess the team's capacity not just in terms of technical skill, but in our ability to absorb the specific friction associated with the choice. It allowed us to be transparent with stakeholders about the trade-offs we were making: if we accepted a tight schedule, we knew we weren't advancing the technology, but we conserved budget; if we pushed the technology, we were explicitly investing in the team's growth and accepting a longer development timeline.

Learning from What Actually Happened

The approach I finally chose wasn't the one I would have selected based purely on analysis. It worked, but not exactly as predicted. The real benefit came from learning lessons during implementation. We gained insights about our processes, team capabilities, and system interactions that no amount of upfront analysis could have provided.

When we navigated the unknowns of the chosen strategy—especially regarding the integration of new features—we discovered that our greatest vulnerabilities weren't where the analysis predicted. The process of testing the hardware under real-world conditions exposed where our assumptions about team skill levels and component interfaces were overly optimistic.

We found that the real benefit of choosing a risk strategy lies in this continuous feedback loop. When we encountered unexpected performance shortfalls with the innovative design, we learned how to iterate rapidly and troubleshoot as a team. When schedule pressures hit the proven technology approach, we learned how to better prioritize tasks and protect our core talent from burnout. Those hands-on insights informed every subsequent decision. They taught us that choosing a risk profile is not just about avoiding failure; it is an active laboratory for system-level learning that makes future projects significantly more successful than if we had stuck with purely theoretical optimization.

When It Goes Wrong:
The Extended Design Review

Not every compromise decision works out well. I remember a situation where we spent months in extended design reviews, trying to find the perfect balance between technical performance and programmatic constraints, and ended up with the worst of both worlds.

We were designing the computer network system for the spacecraft. The network is a complex, multi-layered system that needs multiple levels of redundancy and safety. The current computers and networking hardware couldn't handle the higher data loads we were projecting, so we needed to upgrade everything while maintaining all our reliability requirements.

On paper, we had multiple options that looked viable. We couldn't verify any of them without investing in demo hardware, and our budget was already stretched thin. So we ended up in a cycle of constant iteration, trying to optimize our way to the perfect solution.

Week after week, we'd present updated designs to a room full of stakeholders: our team, the customer, various hardware manufacturers, and networking experts from the company's Technical Fellows program. Each review brought new justifications for why this approach was better, new cost structures to evaluate, new trade-offs to consider.

We kept expanding the option space instead of narrowing it. Every week brought new alternatives to consider, new optimizations to explore, new trade studies to complete. We'd see other implementations that offered more future capability, or would be more modular, or had some other feature that appealed to different team members.

Meanwhile, time was running out. We needed to procure, qualify, and build hardware ahead of the next launch window. We were so focused on finding the optimal solution that we lost sight of finding a workable solution. Eventually, the customer tired of our endless iterating. They forced our hand to the network design we have now because it was good enough and they needed a decision now.

We found a solution that solved the immediate problem, but it offered little room for future expansion. Which means we'll be back at this same decision point again in the future, probably sooner than we'd like.

In trying to avoid compromising on the perfect solution, we ended up with a compromise that satisfied no one. We'd solved for analysis instead of outcomes, and the extended decision-making process had constrained our options rather than expanding them.

Sometimes, avoiding compromise results in a worse outcome imposed by circumstances beyond your control. When you refuse to make the necessary trade-offs yourself, you abdicate your authority and hand your agency over to external deadlines or stakeholders. True leadership means stepping into the discomfort of an imperfect choice rather than waiting for the decision to be made by default. It serves as a stark reminder that analysis is a tool to inform action, not a substitute for it, and that a workable decision executed on time is almost always superior to a perfect one that arrives too late.

Coaching Conversations: Teaching Others to Navigate Trade-offs

One of my responsibilities as a chief engineer is preparing other technical leaders to make these complex decisions. This means helping them understand that technical leadership requires a different kind of thinking than individual contribution.

I remember coaching one of our emerging engineers through their first major design decision. They came to me with a detailed analysis showing why Approach A was technically superior to Approach B in every measurable way.

"Okay," I said. "Now tell me why you might choose Approach B anyway."

The look on their face was worth the price of admission. "Why would I choose the worse technical solution?"

"Because," I explained, "this work means optimizing for mission success and technical performance. What factors beyond pure technical merit might matter for this decision?"

We spent the next hour exploring all the dimensions of the decision that weren't captured in the technical analysis: team capabilities, schedule constraints, supplier relationships, customer preferences, risk tolerance, integration complexity.

By the end of that conversation, they understood that the "worse" technical solution might be the better decision. That's when I knew they were ready to make real technical leadership decisions.

The Human Cost of Technical Decisions

Every technical decision affects people, and skilled technical leaders learn to account for the human impact alongside the technical implications.

Impact on Your Team

When you choose the pragmatic path over the optimal path, how does that affect team morale? Some engineers will understand the broader constraints and support the decision. Others may feel you're asking them to build something they're not proud of.

I've learned to have explicit conversations about this tension, "I know this isn't the solution you would choose if you were optimizing purely for technical performance. Here's why I believe it's the right choice for the mission, and here's how we can use this experience to build better solutions in the future."

Impact on Future Capability

Does this decision help or hurt the team's technical development? Choosing easy solutions consistently can atrophy your team's ability to tackle harder problems. Choosing impossible solutions can destroy confidence and credibility.

The sweet spot is in finding challenges that stretch your team's capabilities without breaking them.

Impact on Stakeholder Relationships

How does this decision affect trust with customers, program management, and other stakeholders? Technical decisions that seem arbitrary or poorly reasoned can damage relationships that take years to rebuild.

Stakeholders can usually accept technical compromises if they understand the reasoning behind them and trust that the decision-maker has their interests in mind.

Reflection Framework: When Perfect Becomes the Enemy of Progress

The hardest decisions in technical leadership are rarely between right and wrong—they're between different versions of "good enough," each with trade-offs that matter to different stakeholders.

Consider Your Recent Technical Decisions

What factors in your decision space do you treat as non-negotiable that might be opportunities to change? Sometimes we turn preferences into requirements without realizing it, which limits our ability to find creative solutions.

When you argue for the "perfect" technical solution, what constraints are you ignoring? Budget, schedule, team capabilities, and stakeholder relationships are all part of the engineering problem, not obstacles to it.

How do your compromise decisions affect your team's confidence and growth? Consistently choosing easy solutions can atrophy your team's capabilities, while impossible solutions destroy credibility.

What invisible constraints might you be missing that affect decision outcomes? Organizational politics, supplier relationships, customer preferences, and regulatory requirements often shape what's possible more than technical analysis does.

One Thing to Try This Week

Before presenting your next technical recommendation, list all the constraints you're operating within. Don't forget the non-technical constraints like schedule, personnel availability, and contract clauses. Ask yourself, "What am I optimizing for?" and "What would I choose if all current options were off the table?" Sometimes the best solutions emerge when you reframe the problem rather than solving it as initially presented.

When Everyone Is Right
(And That's the Problem)

The framework I eventually developed for complex technical decisions emerged from a crisis that had nothing to do with engineering perfectionism and everything to do with stakeholder frustration.

We were six weeks into what should have been a routine design review cycle when everything exploded. The customer wanted more redundancy. The safety team demanded additional testing. The budget office questioned every line item. The scheduling team said we were already behind. Our suppliers were threatening delays. Senior management asked why a "simple" component selection took so long. Each group had completely valid concerns. Each group was absolutely right about its specific area of expertise. Their collective "rightness" paralyzed our ability to make any decision at all.

I found myself in meeting after meeting where smart people presented compelling arguments for mutually exclusive approaches. The safety engineer would explain why we needed extra redundancy, which made perfect sense until the budget analyst explained why that would kill the program. The customer would describe their requirements, which seemed reasonable until the supplier explained why they were technically impossible within our timeline.

This was an emotional architecture problem dressed up as a technical one. Each stakeholder operated from their own definition of success, their own risk tolerance, their own constraints. I needed to design conversations that could surface those underlying priorities and architect solutions that addressed everyone's core concerns.

No Longer the Referee

During a long and painful stakeholder meeting, I watched six different groups essentially talk past each other for two hours. Each person solved a different version of the problem based on their professional perspective and organizational constraints.

Afterward, I realized I'd been approaching these situations completely wrong. I'd been trying to serve as a referee, determining which stakeholder was "right" and which concerns could be dismissed. What I should have been doing was serving as a translator, helping each group understand what the others were trying to protect.

That's when I developed a different approach to multi-stakeholder technical decisions. Instead of starting with the technical options and trying to convince people to accept one, I started by understanding what each stakeholder was trying to accomplish.

The Questions

Over the next several months, I developed a set of questions that helped me navigate these complex stakeholder dynamics more effectively. Not a rigid process, but a way of thinking that ensured I understood the full landscape before trying to find solutions.

Getting genuinely curious about perspectives I initially dismissed became my first tool. When the budget office challenged our component selection, instead of defending our technical analysis, I asked, "Help me understand what financial constraints are driving this concern." That conversation revealed funding uncertainties that completely altered our approach to the decision timeline.

Learning to listen for the concerns people couldn't express directly became equally important. When our supplier kept questioning our specifications, they weren't being difficult— they were trying to warn us about manufacturing challenges they couldn't admit to without looking incompetent. Once I understood what they were worried about, we could address the underlying problems.

Developing empathy for constraints I didn't share opened new possibilities. The customer's "unreasonable" demands made perfect sense when I understood the political pressure they were under from their own management. The safety team's "excessive" requirements were driven by lessons learned from previous failures I knew nothing about.

Questioning assumptions that seemed obviously true often revealed hidden flexibility. Our schedule constraints felt fixed until we discovered that moving certain milestones by two weeks would align better with other program dependencies. Our budget limitations had flexibility we hadn't explored because no one had asked the right questions.

Realigning around shared priorities instead of competing positions became the key to breakthrough solutions. Everyone wanted the program to succeed. Everyone wanted to deliver capability that mattered. Once we focused on those shared goals instead of defending individual positions, creative solutions emerged naturally.

Preventing a Program Disaster

These questions really helped when we faced a supplier crisis that threatened to derail our entire schedule. Our primary supplier had manufacturing problems they'd been hiding for months. Our backup supplier couldn't meet our specifications. Our customer was threatening contract penalties if we missed our delivery date.

Each stakeholder group had a different solution, and each solution created problems for everyone else. The traditional approach would have been to pick the least bad option and force everyone to live with it.

Instead, I spent some time having individual conversations with each stakeholder group, not to defend any technical approach, but to understand what they were trying to accomplish and what constraints they were operating within.

Curiosity revealed that the customer's penalty threats were driven by their own schedule pressures with their end users. They had more flexibility in the delivery date than anyone realized, but they needed confidence that we could hit whatever date we committed to.

Listening uncovered that we had not explored our backup supplier's capabilities because we wrote our original requirements around our primary supplier's approach. They couldn't meet our specifications as written, but they could deliver equivalent functionality through a different technical path.

Empathy helped me understand that our safety team's resistance to the backup supplier wasn't technical stubbornness. They were genuinely concerned about validating a completely different approach within our remaining schedule.

Assumption testing revealed that several of our "fixed" requirements were derived from implementation approaches rather than fundamental mission needs. When we focused on what we needed to accomplish rather than how we'd originally planned to accomplish it, more options became viable.

Realignment around shared priorities led to a solution none of us had initially considered: split the delivery into two phases, with the backup supplier providing a reduced-capability system for initial operations while we qualified the advanced approach for later deployment.

This felt like a compromise, but it was creative problem-solving that emerged from understanding what everyone was trying to protect.

Teaching Others to Navigate Stakeholder Complexity

When I work with emerging technical leaders facing similar multi-stakeholder challenges, I focus on helping them develop curiosity about perspectives they don't initially understand.

"Before you dismiss that concern as unreasonable," I'll say, "spend some time understanding what constraints that person is operating within. What pressures are they managing that you might not see?"

"Instead of defending your technical position, ask questions about what success looks like from their perspective. What are they trying to accomplish? What are they trying to avoid?"

"Look for the shared priorities underneath the competing positions. Where does everyone want the same outcome?"

The most effective technical leaders stop trying to win stakeholder arguments and start building conditions where the best technical solutions can emerge from collaborative problem-solving rather than positional negotiation.

Playbook: Making Technical Compromises That Serve the Mission

When You Have the Perfect Solution That's Too Expensive

You worked hard on your technical analysis. It shows an optimal approach, but it would blow the budget and likely get the program cancelled.

Watch for stakeholders who don't understand the real budget constraints, perfectionism disguised as technical necessity, or hidden funding sources you haven't explored.

Frame the real choice clearly: "We can pursue the perfect solution and risk program cancellation or implement a good solution that keeps us moving forward."

Identify what aspects are negotiable: "What parts of the optimal solution are most critical, and what could we defer to future iterations?"

Plan for evolution rather than abandonment: "How can we design the practical solution to enable upgrades toward the optimal solution later?"

Communicate trade-offs without losing credibility: "Here's what we're gaining and what we're giving up with this approach."

Realize you may not get everything you want in your proposal. Be clear and realistic in communicating the risk/benefit trade you're asking from program management.

When Your Team Wants Technical Perfection

Your engineers are pushing for the most technically elegant solution even though it's not practical within current constraints.

Watch for teams that don't trust you, a reliance on technical excellence over compromise, constraints that feel arbitrary rather than real, or situations where the compromise is too significant.

Honor their technical judgment first: "I appreciate your commitment to technical excellence. Help me understand what we'd lose with a more constrained approach."

Share the context they might not see: "Here's how technical decisions affect program viability and mission success."

Reframe constraints as learning opportunities: "How can we use this project to build capability for future technical challenges?"

Create development paths for the future: "What skills would we need to tackle the optimal solution on the next program?"

Working to communicate risks and options will be more successful than getting defensive or accusatory. Where a compromise is required, everyone will feel a little disappointed.

When Analysis Never Ends

Your team keeps finding new options to consider and can't converge on a decision because there might be an even better solution.

Watch for teams avoiding the responsibility of making imperfect decisions, genuine technical risks that need more analysis, or your own tendency to enable endless analysis.

Set clear decision boundaries: "We need to choose by this date to stay on track. What information do we need to make a good decision?"

Define what *good enough* means: "What level of confidence do we need to move forward, and what risks are acceptable?"

Focus on reversibility: "How could we adjust course if we learn something that changes our assessment?"

Emphasize learning value: "What will we learn by implementing this solution that we can't learn by analyzing it further?"

This is an area where I struggle. It seems important to get all the data or to do *one more analysis*. You don't want to leave an optimization on the table. Better is the enemy of good enough. Returning to your requirements or your performance parameters can keep you from over-designing and over-analyzing.

When Stakeholders Have Competing Priorities

Different groups want mutually exclusive technical approaches, and you need to find a path that serves the mission.

Watch for groups talking past each other, underlying concerns that aren't being expressed directly, or your own bias toward one stakeholder over others.

Map out what each group is trying to protect: "Help me understand what success looks like from your perspective."

Look for shared goals underneath competing positions: "What do we all want to accomplish here?"

Find creative alternatives that address underlying concerns: "What if we approached this problem differently?"

Build solutions that give each group something they need: "How can we address your primary concern while managing theirs?"

If you can bring all the stakeholders together in the same conversation, this often resolves the issue quickly. When that's not possible, be deliberate about clearly communicating each perspective so you don't bias decisions. Uncovering the hidden agendas is important to finding points of compromise.

When Technical Constraints Conflict With Business Reality

It's tough to negotiate between science and business, but sometimes the physics or engineering requirements genuinely conflict with schedule, budget, or organizational capabilities.

Watch for preferences disguised as technical requirements, business constraints that aren't as fixed as they appear, or risks that are genuinely unacceptable for mission success.

Acknowledge the genuine tension: "This is a real conflict between what's technically required and what's practically possible."

Explore the technical floor: "What's the minimum performance we absolutely cannot compromise on?"

Investigate constraint flexibility: "Which constraints are fixed, and which ones might have some flexibility?"

Plan risk mitigation: "If we accept this technical compromise, how do we manage the risks it creates?"

Curiosity is your friend in this situation. Ask questions, look to understand why there's a conflict, try to uncover where there's room to shift.

When Your Team Resists Necessary Compromises

If your technically sound team is struggling to accept solutions that feel suboptimal, even when those solutions serve the mission better, try these options.

Watch for dismissing concerns about "settling," treating resistance as stubbornness rather than professional identity conflict, or making decisions without reaching team understanding and buy-in.

Build space for their concerns: "I know this feels like we're compromising our standards. What's most troubling about this approach?"

Reframe the optimization problem: "How do we define technical excellence when we're optimizing for mission success within real constraints?"

Design shared ownership: "What would need to be true for all of us to feel good about this approach, even if it's not our first choice?"

Create learning infrastructure: "How will we capture what we learn from this compromise to inform better decisions next time?"

It can feel like parenting in these situations. You're trying to explain the logic and the reasoning to people who are resisting your efforts.

The Long Game of Technical Decision-Making

The decisions to choose pragmatic paths often feel terrible in the moment. Months later, when you're testing hardware and generating real data while others are still analyzing their perfect solutions, the wisdom of pragmatic compromise becomes clear.

The experience of building and testing those "suboptimal" components taught us things we never would have learned from analysis alone. Problems we hadn't anticipated. Performance characteristics the models didn't predict. Integration challenges that became apparent only during assembly. That real-world learning informed the design of the next-generation system, which was significantly better than what we could have designed based on analysis alone. Sometimes, the path to technical excellence runs through technical compromise.

In the next chapter, we'll explore how to prevent the conflicts and crises that force these difficult trade-offs—how upstream thinking and proactive problem-solving can expand your decision space and reduce the frequency of "choose between bad options" scenarios.

The Emotional Labor Tax: When "Whatever You Want" Becomes Toxic

Chapter 6

AFTER A DAY of meetings in Washington, DC, I conversed with a colleague about dinner plans. "Where should we go tonight?" I asked, scrolling through restaurant options on my phone. "Oh, I'm easy," came the familiar response. "Whatever you want. I'm fine with anything." (This colleague had access to the same Google search of "restaurants near me" that I did.) His statement sounded reasonable. Accommodating. Even generous. He let me choose since I was the one doing the research.

I heard something different. *I want you to bear the risk for this decision. I want you to manage my satisfaction with whatever we choose. I want you to do the emotional work of considering everyone's preferences, dietary restrictions, and potential complaints, while I stay comfortable by avoiding any responsibility for the outcome.*

What should have been a simple dinner choice had become an invisible transaction where I absorbed all the decision-making complexity while he maintained plausible deniability if things didn't work out perfectly.

This really set off my internal radar. We were no longer having a collaborative discussion. He was dumping the emotional labor of decision making and disguising it as flexibility. I saw the blueprint of our team for what it really was: a lopsided structure where I was the only load-bearing wall. While I was busy trying to be *supportive*, I had actually designed a system that let everyone else opt out of the hard work of choosing. I was carrying the weight, and they were just along for the ride.

The same invisible transaction that frustrated me over dinner choices played out in so many other places in my professional life. Team members would present me with problems while subtly declining to engage with solutions. Stakeholders would ask for my recommendations while remaining at a defensible distance if things went wrong. What I'd dismissed as normal team dynamics suddenly looked like systematic emotional labor dumping—and I was the designated repository.

Origin Story: Journaling for the Win

Later that evening, I journaled about why such a simple exchange had felt so frustrating. As I wrote, I saw the pattern that had been invisible to me for years. He wasn't acknowledging my superior restaurant-selection skills. He was handing me the emotional labor of managing the decision, and by extension, the responsibility for his satisfaction with whatever I chose. If the restaurant turned out to be disappointing, he could mentally distance himself from the choice while I carried the weight of having *gotten it wrong*.

That journaling session was a revelation because it helped me recognize this dynamic in many other contexts. The *what's for dinner* question was a source of frustration in every relationship

I'd ever had. It appeared with the *whatever you think is best* responses in technical meetings. Suddenly, the *you're the expert* deferrals sounded like respect but felt like burden-shifting.

For years, I'd been absorbing this emotional labor without realizing it was happening. I thought being helpful meant taking on whatever responsibility people wanted to give me. I thought being a good leader meant making others comfortable by carrying their anxiety, their decision-making burden, and their risk of being wrong.

Once I could name the pattern, I saw it elsewhere. I saw team members deferring decisions to avoid the risk of being wrong. More stakeholders asked me to "handle" difficult conversations they didn't want to have. Colleagues stopped by my office to drop complex problems on my desk, assuming I would figure out both the technical solution and how to manage everyone's feelings about implementing it. I understood that emotional labor dumping was systematically undermining the emotional architecture I was trying to build. When people dump decision-making responsibility, you can't create the collaborative intelligence that technical challenges require.

I stumbled across sociologist Arlie Hochschild's[9] work while looking for an explanation for my own exhaustion. She studied flight attendants in the 80s, but she might as well have been studying lead engineers. She called it 'emotional labor'—the invisible work of managing everyone's feelings just to keep the flight (or the project) from crashing. Her research revealed that emotional labor involves not simply managing your own emotions, but managing others' emotional experiences—anticipating their

---

9   Hochschild, A. R. (1983). *The Managed Heart: Commercialization of Human Feeling*. University of California Press.

needs, absorbing their anxieties, and taking responsibility for their comfort and satisfaction.

I was experiencing in technical leadership what Hochschild observed in the airline industry. Flight attendants expected to smile, stay calm, and manage emotions even when people were hostile or unreasonable. I was expected to absorb team anxieties about difficult decisions, manage stakeholder emotions around disappointing news, and take responsibility for everyone's comfort with outcomes, all while maintaining a composed, competent exterior. The same invisible expectation that flight attendants should manage the emotional climate of the cabin was operating in our conference rooms and project meetings. I realized I had a major design flaw in my leadership. I thought I was being a supportive 'architect,' but I'd built a one-way street. All the messy, uncomfortable human complexity was flowing straight to my desk, while everyone else got a free pass on the hard work of actually collaborating.

The Hidden Transaction: When "You Decide" Isn't Deference

There was another pattern I noticed that was more subtle and more damaging than obvious conflict: the moments when people handed me their emotional labor while calling it respect for my expertise.

I used to beam when a colleague said, "I'll defer to your judgment." I thought it was respect. It took years to realize they weren't tipping their hat to my expertise—they were handing me the grenade so they wouldn't be holding it when it went off.

For the longest time, I thought these responses meant people respected my expertise. Someone saying, "You're the engineer, whatever you think is best," felt like validation that I'd earned their trust. It took me an embarrassingly long time to realize what had happened. They weren't deferring to my expertise. They were bypassing the emotional architecture I was trying to build. Real collaborative systems require shared ownership of uncertainty and risk. When people dump their anxiety about being wrong, they're opting out of the very engagement that makes technical teams effective.

The Project Planning Trap

The most exhausting emotional labor dump I experienced happened during what was supposed to be a collaborative project planning session. We were working on resource allocation for the next quarter, and I'd asked each team lead to come prepared with their priorities and resource needs. As I went around the table and asked each lead to share their recommendations, I got variations of, "I don't really have a good plan because I didn't want to redo it when you decide." I was frustrated when a manager said, "Whatever you think makes the most sense." I could feel my neck getting hot as another told me, "You know the big picture better than we do."

My annoyance here was probably more visible than I liked. I sensed my managers felt my disappointment, and they weren't sure why. I saw a room full of people who wanted me to make difficult trade-offs so they wouldn't have to advocate for their own teams' needs or risk disappointing stakeholders. They were avoiding being a problem.

Every time I tried to draw out their actual preferences—"What would happen if we delayed Project X by two weeks?"—I got responses like "That's probably fine" or "We can make it work." Nobody wanted to be the person who said their project was more important than someone else's, or that a proposed timeline was unrealistic, or that they needed resources they weren't sure they deserved. Instead of a planning session where team leads took ownership of their requirements and we negotiated trade-offs transparently, I tried to read minds, guess at hidden concerns, and make decisions based on incomplete information while everyone else stayed safely non-committal.

By the time the meeting ended, I had made the final decision about resource allocation and prepared to address any unspoken disappointment others might have with my choice. More importantly, the impact of that resource planning fell solely on my shoulders. If this didn't work, it was going to be up to me to resolve the problem. My team got to preserve their relationships with each other by avoiding any direct advocacy, and I absorbed all the interpersonal complexity of competing priorities. I had failed to design a system where people felt safe advocating for their teams' needs. Instead, I had accidentally built a dynamic where avoiding conflict felt safer than engaging in productive disagreement.

The Real Cost of "Whatever You Want"

Every organization has what I call an *Emotional Architect*. This is someone who absorbs complexity, anticipates consequences, and manages the group's emotional weather. If you're reading this book, there's a good chance that's you.

One night, while working the third shift as a satellite operator in the Air Force, I spoke with a colleague about my frustration over how some changes were happening. I didn't agree with the plan and felt like my concerns were being ignored. I knew the changes would cause a lot more work for me, and I didn't enjoy looking forward to that additional burden. I was concerned that our work quality would suffer. He said, "You care too much to put out an inferior product. This will be fine, just different. You don't have to carry all the weight because you have a team." I didn't understand the depth of his observation when he said it. He saw and gave language to my skills as an emotional architect—a role I wouldn't fully comprehend until years later, when I began my work as a leadership mentor.

The cost isn't operational. It's relational. Each time someone says, "Whatever you want," they're adding an invisible rock to your backpack. You're not just making decisions—you're managing other people's satisfaction with those decisions. You're not just solving technical problems—you're absorbing the emotional risk of being wrong. You're not just leading projects—you're carrying everyone else's responsibility for outcomes.

Recognizing this pattern changes how you perceive workplace interactions. It echoes through familiar scenarios: project planning becomes, "You're so much better at thinking through details, so you figure out the timeline." Stakeholder management morphs into, "You have such a good relationship with the customer, so you handle that conversation." Technical disputes reduce to, "You understand the implications better than I do, so you make the call." These seemingly innocuous statements reveal a deeper dynamic: people are handing you the decisions *and* their full emotional weight.

Shared ownership looks different. Instead of "Whatever you think is best," it sounds like, "I'm leaning toward Option A because of X concern, but I want to hear your thoughts on the Y risk." Instead of "You decide—you know more about this," it becomes, "I don't have enough information to be confident, but here's what I'm worried about." Partnership means being willing to say, "I think we should go with B, but I'll own raising my concerns with the customer if that's the direction we go."

You're not aiming for perfection from your team. You're aiming for co-authorship—a shared pursuit of excellence where managing complexity is everyone's job, not one person's burden.

There is a massive weight shift when someone says, "I'm leaning toward A" instead of "Whatever you want." In that moment, the risk is shared. I'm no longer jumping alone; we're jumping together. Instead of being a superhero who can carry everyone's emotional load, your role is to architect systems where the load can be more equitably shared.

How This Shows Up Everywhere: The Universal Burden

The emotional labor dumping patterns I saw in my professional life didn't stay only at work. They were everywhere, woven into the fabric of most of my relationships.

In romantic relationships, it showed up as the exhausting dance of being the person who remembers birthdays, manages social calendars, and somehow becomes responsible for both people's emotional well-being. "You're so much better at keeping track of these things," partners would say, as if relationship maintenance was a skill I'd been born with rather than labor I'd been socialized to perform.

I'd plan date nights and manage my partner's satisfaction with those plans. I remembered his mother's birthday, as well as found the appropriate gift and managed his anxiety about whether she'd like it. The emotional work was doing all these things and carrying the responsibility for how well they worked out.

With friendships, it manifested as being the person everyone called during crises but who rarely felt comfortable reaching out when I needed support. I'd become the designated emotional processing center for my social circle, absorbing everyone's relationship drama, career anxieties, and family conflicts while learning to present my life as perpetually manageable.

Even in family dynamics, I noticed the pattern. I was the one who planned holiday gatherings, managed the complex logistics of getting everyone together, and somehow became responsible for ensuring that everyone had a good time. If there was family tension, I managed other people's discomfort rather than addressing the actual issues.

The insidious part was how good it felt to be needed, to be seen as capable and reliable. There's a particular satisfaction that comes from being the person others turn to when things get complicated. That satisfaction comes at the cost of carrying emotional labor that should be distributed more equitably.

This pattern was especially tiring because it went mostly unnoticed. People weren't consciously deciding to dump their emotional work on me. They were responding to social conditioning that taught them that certain people (often women, often people who'd demonstrated emotional competence) were naturally better at managing social complexity. Natural aptitude doesn't mean infinite capacity. Being good at emotional work doesn't mean you should be responsible for everyone else's emotional work. Being willing to help doesn't mean you should become the default repository for whatever emotional labor others want to avoid.

Noticing this recurring pattern everywhere made me ask myself a tough question: *was my worth to others mostly about how much emotional labor I was willing to take on?* How might my relationships change if that responsibility were distributed more fairly? Looking back, I realize I was the designated 'pressure valve' for everyone else's anxiety. It's a lonely place to be.

Dietary restrictions provide a perfect example of how this gets rationalized. Just because someone has specific dietary needs doesn't mean they should automatically become responsible for managing everyone else's food decisions. They already carry the cognitive load of navigating their own restrictions. Making them responsible for everyone else's satisfaction is adding unnecessary emotional labor.

The person with dietary restrictions knows exactly what they can and can't eat. They've already done the mental work of figuring out the options. When the group automatically defers to them for all food decisions, they're now responsible for everyone's happiness with the choice.

The View from Outside: Conscious vs. Unconscious Dumping

An uncomfortable insight I gained when learning about emotional labor dumping was acknowledging that I, too, have sometimes contributed to this pattern. While I was often the recipient of emotional labor dumps, I had to acknowledge that I sometimes initiated them too. I'd become more conscious of when I was doing it, which meant I could catch myself and course-correct. It also meant I had to confront the ways I contributed to the dynamics I was criticizing.

I noticed I was most likely to dump emotional labor when I was overwhelmed or when I encountered situations outside my comfort zone. During particularly stressful periods, I'd ask my partner to "handle" social planning because I didn't have the bandwidth to manage the coordination and everyone's preferences. When dealing with complex interpersonal conflicts, I'd sometimes defer to colleagues who were "better at that kind of thing" rather than developing my own skills for navigating those conversations.

Most people who dump emotional labor aren't malicious about it. They've learned someone else will handle the complexity, so they've stopped working on their own capacity to manage it. They say, "Whatever you want" because they genuinely believe they're being accommodating. They've learned you'll make good decisions, so why not let you decide? They don't want to be responsible if the choice doesn't work out. They're uncomfortable with the uncertainty of decision-making, or they've never been required to build their own decision-making skills in these areas.

These people can usually learn to recognize the pattern once you point it out. They didn't realize the impact their deference had on you, and they're willing to grow their own capacity once they understand what's needed.

There's a smaller group of people who dump emotional labor consciously and systematically. These are the people who've figured out that if they consistently avoid responsibility, someone else will pick it up. They've learned to frame their avoidance as personality traits, "I'm not good with details," or "I'm more of a big picture person," or "You're so much better at this than I am."

You can identify chronic emotional labor dumpers by their patterns: they always have explanations for why they can't handle something, they consistently position themselves as victims of circumstances, they never develop competence in areas where someone else will do the work, they take credit for successes and distance themselves from failures, and they resist any attempt to build their capacity for handling complexity.

With these people, trying to build their capability is often futile. They've invested in helplessness as a strategy for avoiding responsibility. Your choice is whether to continue enabling this pattern or to stop volunteering for their emotional labor.

When It Goes Wrong:
The Management Expectation Trap

Sometimes emotional labor dumping becomes so embedded in organizational culture that it's treated as part of your job description, even when it's not.

I remember a period when I was consistently asked to "handle" difficult conversations with stakeholders, manage team dynamics that other leaders found challenging, and take on projects that required navigating complex organizational politics. At first, I was flattered. This felt like recognition of my capabilities and trust in my judgment.

Over time, I realized I had become the organization's emotional labor repository. Anything that required managing feelings, building consensus, or navigating interpersonal complexity automatically landed on my desk.

The pattern became clear during a particularly challenging project when two engineering leads couldn't agree on a technical approach. Instead of requiring them to work through their disagreement themselves, their manager asked me to "facilitate a solution" because I was "good with people." I spent hours in separate conversations with each of them, essentially doing the conflict resolution work that they needed to learn to do themselves. Meanwhile, my own technical deliverables sat waiting.

My breaking point came when I was asked to "smooth things over" with a customer who was frustrated about delays caused by decisions I hadn't been involved in making. Management asked me to manage the emotional consequences of other people's technical choices. That's when I realized accepting emotional labor dumps, even when they're framed as recognition of your skills, can undermine your ability to do your primary job effectively.

This insight changed my approach to interactions where people were trying to hand me responsibility that belonged to them. Instead of accepting the labor dump or bluntly refusing it, I learned to redirect those conversations in ways that built their capability while protecting my capacity.

The Organizational Cost of Emotional Labor Dumping

When emotional labor gets concentrated in one or two people, it creates organizational vulnerabilities that can destroy even well-intentioned teams. When emotional labor gets dumped onto a few people, they eventually burn out and leave—taking with them all the institutional knowledge, relationship management, and coordination that kept things functioning.

The organizational vulnerabilities this creates are severe:

Decision-making suffers because you're not getting the right information when people don't speak up. Silent team members often have crucial insights about technical risks, customer needs, or implementation challenges, but if they've learned to defer all decisions to the emotional labor carriers, that information never reaches the people making choices. The correction is structural: create explicit decision frameworks that require input from multiple team members before a choice is finalized, so participation becomes the process rather than a courtesy.

Key player burnout becomes inevitable because the people carrying everyone else's emotional labor eventually reach their limits and either leave the organization or pull back dramatically from their coordinating role. When they do, the team suddenly discovers how much they were depending on someone else to manage the relational and organizational aspects of their work. The path out requires making that invisible work visible—naming it, assigning it, and distributing it deliberately before the inevitable exit forces the reckoning.

Performance gets delayed when issues are uncovered later because someone didn't raise concerns early. If team members are in the habit of deferring difficult conversations or avoiding challenging discussions, problems that could have been addressed quickly often compound into crises. Teams can interrupt this pattern by normalizing early escalation—treating "I see a potential problem" as a contribution rather than a complaint.

Creativity and innovation stagnate because the people with the best ideas have learned that contributing means taking on additional responsibility for coordination and relationship management. It becomes easier to stay quiet than to suggest improvements that might require emotional labor to implement. When teams redistribute that coordination burden so that good ideas don't automatically become personal projects, the ideas flow again.

When a team has a healthy emotional labor distribution, the contrast is striking. There isn't a single person or small group managing all the relational aspects of the team. Difficult conversations, morale building, team assignments, and decision-making are shared responsibilities. Team members don't automatically defer to the highest-paid person or the most senior engineer. Everyone has clear job responsibilities and performance expectations that include contributing to the team's emotional and relational health.

In healthy teams, when someone asks, "What do you think we should do?" the response isn't "Whatever you decide" but rather genuine engagement with the decision-making process. When problems arise, multiple people step forward to help solve them rather than looking around for the designated problem-solver to handle it. Teams that distribute emotional labor effectively can handle more complex challenges, adapt more quickly to changing circumstances, and maintain their performance even when key individuals are unavailable. These teams build deep resilience and are far more successful.

Building Emotional Labor Equity

After months of recognizing how much emotional labor I was absorbing, I needed to find a more sustainable path. I was deeply engaged in caring about team dynamics and being helpful. I didn't want to stop that, but I needed other people to carry their share of the load. That meant changing not just what I did, but how I showed up in the moments when someone tried to hand me their responsibility.

Creating Distributed Development Opportunities

Instead of always being the person who handles difficult conversations, create opportunities for others to develop these skills. When a stakeholder discussion needs to happen, say, "I'd like you to lead this conversation. I'll be there for support, but you drive the interaction." When conflicts emerge, try saying, "This situation needs resolution. What's your approach? How can I support you in having that conversation?" For team dynamics issues, ask, "The interpersonal dynamics on this project need attention. What do you think would help?"

The goal is to build others' capacity rather than handling everything yourself. This requires resisting the urge to jump in when things get uncomfortable and instead coaching people through their own learning process.

Setting Clear Boundaries Around Dumping

It's incredibly hard to stay quiet when someone brings you a problem you know you can fix in five minutes. But every time I said, "I'll handle it," I was stealing their opportunity to learn. Now, I try to lead with a question: "I've got thoughts, but what's your first move here?"

Boundaries aren't about being unhelpful. They're about creating conditions where others grow their own capabilities. When you consistently solve interpersonal problems for others, you prevent them from developing the skills they need to handle similar situations independently.

Recognizing and Rewarding Emotional Labor Contributions

When people do take on emotional architecture work, recognize and celebrate it explicitly. Saying, "Thank you for facilitating that difficult team conversation," or "I appreciate how you managed the stakeholder dynamics on that project," or "Your conflict resolution skills helped us move forward," does more than acknowledge one person. It signals to the entire team that this work has value.

Recognition helps people understand that emotional architecture isn't a mysterious talent that some people have and others don't. It's a set of learnable skills that benefit from practice and feedback, just like technical skills. When you celebrate these contributions, you're modeling that interpersonal competence is as valuable as technical competence for organizational success.

Breaking the Cycle:
How to Stop Enabling
Emotional Labor Dumping

The key to changing these dynamics is recognizing you have more power than you think. Every time someone tries to hand you their emotional labor, you have a choice about whether to accept it.

I used to think I was just being a 'giver,' but then I came across Adam Grant's[10] work and realized I was actually being a 'doormat.' He makes a distinction that changed my perspective. He found 'givers' who help others indiscriminately often burn out and perform worse than both 'takers' (who focus on getting) and 'matchers' (who balance giving and receiving). The most successful givers, Grant discovered, are those who give strategically. They help others in ways that build capabilities rather than creating dependencies.

This research validates what I experienced: saying, *whatever you want*, isn't helpful deference—it's dependency creation. When I absorbed everyone else's decision-making anxiety, I wasn't helping them become better leaders. I was helping them stay comfortable with not building those skills themselves.

Start by getting comfortable with redirecting rather than absorbing. When someone says, "Whatever you want," try responding with "I'd like to hear your thoughts first," or "What are you leaning toward?" When they defer a decision to you, ask, "What criteria should we use to decide this?" or "What would need to be true for each option to work well?"

---

10 Grant, A. (2013). *Give and Take: Why Helping Others Drives Our Success*. Viking.

For people who are unconsciously dumping, this redirection often works immediately. They needed prompting to engage their own decision-making capacity. For chronic dumpers, you'll get pushback, "You're so much better at this" or "I don't have a preference." That's when you hold firm, "I'm confident you can think through this. Take a few minutes and let me know what you come up with."

The most important shift is refusing to rescue people from the natural consequences of not building their own capacity. If someone consistently avoids planning, don't step in when their lack of planning creates problems. If someone refuses to engage in decision-making, don't absorb their anxiety when decisions need to be made without their input.

I know this can sound cold. It isn't. You're not withholding help. You're offering a different kind of assistance, the kind that builds competence in capable adults rather than keeping them dependent on yours. That serves everyone better in the long run.

How to Stop Making Others Carry Your Risk

While it's important to recognize when others are dumping emotional labor on you, it's equally crucial to examine your own patterns. If you're reading this book, chances are you've been on both sides of this dynamic. Sometimes you're carrying others' emotional labor, and sometimes unconsciously handing yours off to someone else.

Most emotional labor dumping isn't malicious. It happens because we've learned certain people will step in and handle things when we defer, complain without offering solutions, or claim to be "flexible" about decisions we deeply care about. Recognizing these patterns in yourself—and changing them—is essential for building the kind of collaborative technical teams that can handle complex challenges.

Before You Defer, Ask Yourself

When you catch yourself about to hand off a decision or responsibility, pause and ask yourself, "How am I going to contribute to this solution rather than feeding off the generosity and efforts of others?"

If you're about to say, "Whatever you want," stop. You're not being helpful. You're being emotionally lazy. Take a moment to consider the options and offer your perspective, even if it's not a strong preference.

If you're about to complain about a problem, ask yourself, "Am I offering to be part of the solution, or am I expecting someone else to fix this for me?"

If you're expecting someone else to handle a difficult conversation, ask yourself, "Is this their responsibility, or am I avoiding discomfort by making it their problem?"

How to Take Ownership When You Realize You've Been Dumping

When you recognize that you've been handing off your emotional labor, the most powerful thing you can do is acknowledge it directly and change your behavior going forward.

"I want to apologize for the other day. You asked me to decide, and I offloaded it onto you instead. I want to be more proactive, and I'm going to make a point of taking responsibility for my own choices."

Or, when you need genuine support, "I have a tough conversation coming up, and it would mean a lot to me if I could share my planned approach with you to get any pointers you might have. I'm not asking you to handle it. I want to make sure I'm thinking about it clearly." You're asking for input to improve your own performance, not asking someone else to take over your responsibilities.

When You Feel Pushed to Back Down

This chapter focused on how to respond when others offload their risk onto you. Sometimes, that offloaded risk can be from the people above you. It looks a little different, but the impact is just as big.

It's common in technical teams to have disagreements between program management and technical leaders. Often, the fast, affordable solution comes with unacceptable technical risk. Recently, my program managers wanted to bypass a hardware inspection that would yield important pre-flight data because that inspection wouldn't solve the immediate problem of whether we could use the hardware for flight. The inspection took time and was in the last few weeks before the mission (and two days before Christmas). I was the only voice in the room that said, "If we don't take the time to look at this hardware, we will regret it later. It might not solve our immediate problem, but it will make a big difference after the flight when we're comparing the pre- and post-flight performance." It felt like I'd just dropped a gorilla in the room. I made many people angry. The program manager asked me to join their daily status call the next day to explain my reasons. I stuck to my position, and in the end, the program manager agreed to the inspection.

You won't always get the program managers to agree with you. Sometimes, the superior technical solution is too costly. In those cases, it's important for you to explain the risk they are taking by making this decision. Think ahead of the potential impact on you, your team, or the program and give a detailed perspective. Be kind to your future self. Even if you are pushed into a position you don't like, take the initiative now to reduce the impact. Hopefully, the risk won't materialize, but taking a few steps now can minimize the cleanup. This could be a request for additional resources to mitigate the increased workload. It could be clearly documenting the situation, so you have a clear memory when you recover. You might ask a few people on your team or affiliated teams what it looks like if this doesn't go your way. It's not worth investing a ton of resources into this because the decision is made. It is worth an hour or two to be clear about your assessment of the risk, what is needed to recover, and who the right people are to bring together.

As an emotional architect, your focus is on building your team to show emotional competence. You can't neglect the importance of demonstrating that to your program managers, other technical leaders, and customers. Just as you must be mindful of accepting emotional labor from your team, be vigilant of it being pushed from above.

Reflection Framework: Auditing Your Emotional Labor Load

Emotional labor dumping is often invisible until you look for it systematically. The goal is to identify where you're doing emotional work that should be shared.

Look at This Week's Interactions

What decisions did people consistently defer to you with phrases like "whatever you think is best" or "you're the expert?" Notice the difference between genuinely seeking expertise and avoiding responsibility.

Which conversations did others avoid that automatically ended up on your desk? Planning difficult discussions, managing team tensions, or coordinating between conflicting stakeholders often becomes "your job" with no one deciding it should be.

Who becomes suddenly agreeable when it's time to make difficult decisions? Watch for people who have strong opinions about everything except who should own the risk when things go wrong.

What work gets framed as "you're so good at this" when the subtext is "I don't want to deal with this?" Managing stakeholder emotions, smoothing over conflicts, or handling "difficult" people often gets dumped on whoever has shown they can handle it.

Did you find your managers are pushing additional risk to you and your team? Where do you feel pushed to make a situation work where it clearly doesn't?

One Thing to Try This Week

The next time someone tries to defer a decision to you, respond with, "I value your judgment on this. What's your initial thinking?" If they're willing to adjust regarding something important to them, try asking, "How would this best suit your needs?" Notice both their response and how it feels to redirect the emotional work back to them. If they insist on your accepting their position when it comes with extra work for you, respond with, "This decision will cause a lot of work for my team and puts us in a riskier position. I want to make sure we both understand the impact. When can we talk about the things I'll need to make this work?"

Playbook:
Managing Emotional Labor Dumping

This playbook is a little different because emotional labor is a subject that benefits from a lot of coaching. As you mentor the people on your team, here are some coaching tips to guide you.

It can feel very heavy and weighted down when, as a leader, so much of the team defers to you. In this situation, coach people to draw out responses from others. Say things like, "I'm flattered that you defer the choice to me. It is difficult to carry the weight of decisions, and I'd appreciate your input and buy-in." or "I appreciate your being agreeable. I invited you to this conversation because I value your opinion and expertise, so please share your thoughts."

When people consistently defer decisions to you, address the pattern directly rather than accepting it as respect for your authority.

Instead of taking on the deferred decision, say something like:

1. "I notice you're deferring this decision to me. While I appreciate the trust, I need your thinking on this. What's your initial reaction to these options?"
2. "I value your perspective on this. Before I share my thoughts, what are you seeing that I should consider?"
3. "It sounds like you might have an opinion about this, and you're holding back. I need your expertise and your agreement."
4. "Help me understand—when you say *whatever I think is best*, what are you hoping I'll consider that you might not have mentioned?"

The goal is to create enough discomfort with the dumping pattern that people engage rather than deflect.

Be explicit about the impact by saying, "When decisions get deferred to me consistently, I end up carrying risk that should be shared across the team. I need collaborators. It doesn't help to have people who will go along with whatever I decide."

For decisions that get pushed from above, consider saying, "I understand the importance of [this issue], and I want to make sure we agree on the risk we're accepting. This doesn't come free. Here is the risk I see…"

Some people respond well to this direct feedback and start engaging more actively. Others resist because they prefer the comfort of avoiding responsibility. That tells you something important about their readiness for a real partnership and real leadership.

The Choice Point

That night, scrolling through restaurant options while my dinner companion waited for me to choose "whatever I wanted," I made a different choice than I'd made hundreds of times before. Instead of absorbing the decision-making load, I said, "I need you to participate in this decision. Let's narrow it down together."

The response was telling: a moment of surprise, followed by actual engagement. Suddenly we had a real conversation about what we were both in the mood for, what neighborhoods we wanted to explore, what kind of experience we wanted. The decision became collaborative instead of being dumped.

It was a small moment, but it revealed that people are often capable of carrying their own emotional labor. They just need someone to refuse to carry it for them first.

The Ongoing Choice

Every time someone says "whatever you want," or "you're the expert," or "you handle it better than I would," you have a choice.

You can accept the emotional labor dump because it's easier, or because it feels like recognition of your capabilities. Using it as an opportunity to build capacity in others serves the long-term mission far better than serving the immediate moment.

Building emotional labor literacy takes time and intentional effort. People who've never had to develop these skills need patience and coaching. Organizations that have relied on emotional labor dumping need new expectations and reward systems that recognize when people step into interpersonal challenges rather than deflecting them. The investment is worth it—and it's yours to start.

In the next chapter, we'll explore how breaking free requires learning to think upstream—catching problems before they become emergencies and building systems that prevent failures rather than responding to them heroically.

Fighting Fires vs. Preventing Them: Confessions of a Reformed Crisis Addict

Chapter 7

B Y THIS POINT in my career as chief engineer, I'd developed strong frameworks for building teams and navigating conflict. I was addicted to being needed, which meant I was systematically building dysfunction. Every time I accepted someone else's emotional labor, I designed systems that required my constant intervention rather than building systems that could function independently.

It was my third emergency review board that week. Sitting around the conference room table, watching exhausted engineers present their latest crisis analysis, I felt that familiar cocktail of adrenaline and frustration building in my chest. We were good at diagnosing problems, creating workarounds, and implementing fixes under pressure.

As the conversation swirled, I was asking myself why I was doing this again. All week, I'd been absorbing the emotional labor of decision-making, risk avoidance, and responsibility deflection. I was addicted to the drama of crisis response. I was systematically creating the crises I prided myself on managing.

There's something intoxicating about crisis mode. Your phone buzzes with urgent messages. Senior management wants your input. The team looks to you for solutions. You work late, think fast, save the day. People notice your contributions. They appreciate your expertise. They need you. You feel like a genuine leader.

Sitting in that third emergency meeting, watching my team's energy drain as we fought yet another fire, I had a moment of uncomfortable clarity: we had become so skilled at crisis management that we'd stopped asking why there were so many crises to manage.

Origin Story:
The Air Force Training in Crisis Response

My formative years in spacecraft operations taught me that crisis management was heroic work.

Picture this: a sterile control room filled with humming computers, multiple screens displaying orbital telemetry, and a team of specialists monitoring a fleet of satellites thousands of miles above Earth. Most days were routine—checking systems, logging data, confirming that everything was operating within normal parameters.

Then the alarm would sound. The shrill tone of a 1970s computer terminal cut through the din of the background noise. It was annoying enough that no one wanted to let it continue. We jumped to our feet and ran to silence the terminal while awaiting the news it had for us.

Maybe it was an unexpected power spike. Perhaps a communication anomaly during a critical maneuver. Sometimes it was space weather threatening to disrupt operations. When those moments hit, everything changed. The energy in the room shifted from routine monitoring to focused intensity. Everyone had a role, everyone knew their procedures, and we executed crisis response plans with military precision.

I was good at this work. The rush of solving problems under pressure, the satisfaction of bringing a critical system back online, the recognition that came from being the person who could handle anything. It was intoxicating. I built my identity around being essential during emergencies.

The military environment reinforced this mindset at every level. Rapid response was a virtue. Crisis management was a core competency. Being the person who could save the day showed leadership value. We had detailed contingency plans for every conceivable failure mode, and executing those plans flawlessly under pressure was how you earned respect and advancement.

Moving from military satellite ops to civilian engineering felt like trying to land a plane in a thick fog with no instruments. In the military, my 'enemies' were easy to identify: solar flares, hardware frying in orbit, or a broken uplink. Those were crises of physics. They were loud, they were urgent, and the adrenaline high of fixing them was a drug. But when I got to the civilian world, I realized I was still looking for fires to jump into—only to find out that most 'emergencies' were just poorly managed egos and bad meetings.

What I brought to this role was the same rush-toward-crisis mentality, but now I applied it to problems that were largely self-inflicted. I got the same satisfaction from solving predictable integration failures and schedule conflicts I'd gotten from responding to satellite anomalies.

The critical difference was that these engineering "emergencies" usually stemmed from upstream decisions that could have been made differently. What I didn't initially understand was how to distinguish between necessary crisis response and unnecessary crisis creation—or, more importantly, how to shift from heroic firefighting to systematic fire prevention.

The Seductive Appeal of Being Indispensable

I loved being the person everyone turned to when things went wrong. When a complex failure analysis stumped everyone else, they called me. When stakeholders panicked about a schedule delay, I was pulled into the meeting. When a technical issue threatened the program, I stayed late to find a solution. Being the person who saved the day felt necessary, felt important, and finally felt like leadership.

There's a dark side to being the crisis hero. You need crises to feel valuable. What I didn't realize was that my addiction to crisis heroics kept my entire organization in firefighting mode. I trained my team to design their work around my intervention rather than building systems that could function independently.

I got a little excited when problems emerged that only I could solve. I felt a surge of satisfaction when my expertise saved the day. The addiction was subtle yet powerful. I derived my professional identity from being indispensable during disasters. Like any addiction, it slowly destroyed my team's ability to prevent problems before they became disasters, and ran me ragged, leaving little room for family or a personal life.

The Pattern Recognition Moment

Imagine an organization where we tracked our "firefighting" activities systematically. The irony is so real. With that map in front of me, I saw how we all felt when we handled emergencies and wanted to document our crisis management effectiveness. The data told a different story than I had expected.

Instead of solving each crisis and moving on, we asked a simple question, *what happened upstream that allowed this issue to evolve?* The answers were uncomfortable. They weren't unforeseeable failures. They were natural consequences of upstream decisions that were made without sufficient forethought.

- Design defects often traced back to rushed review cycles where the team felt pressured to move fast rather than taking time to get the right voices in the room, or more insidiously, when the team tried to keep the review small and not consider all the affected aspects of the larger system.
- Integration failures usually started with different teams making incompatible assumptions about interfaces—assumptions that went unquestioned because we were focused on delivery speed rather than communication depth.
- Schedule delays frequently began with optimistic estimates intended to show senior management that we were aggressive about timelines.
- Quality escapes typically originated from procedures that were approved on the fast track without getting input from the people who had to use them, or the engineers responsible for verifying the outcome.

We had become firefighters who were unconsciously setting fires. My crisis addiction created technical problems and slowly undermined the leadership work that enables independent thinking, proactive problem-solving, and collaborative excellence.

How This Shows Up Everywhere: The Over-Functioning Pattern

These crisis addiction patterns from my technical work created a web of dysfunction I mistook for being helpful, even in my personal life.

In couples therapy, my therapist introduced me to the term "over-functioning." It's what happens when one person in a relationship consistently takes on more than their share of emotional and logistical responsibility. The over-functioning partner manages everything from social calendars to emotional processing, while the under-functioning partner learns to rely on that management instead of growing their own capacity.

What I discovered was that over-functioning in relationships and crisis addiction in leadership are the same dysfunction. In both cases, I prevented others from developing their own capabilities by consistently stepping in to handle what they could learn to handle themselves.

Over-functioning in a relationship creates learned helplessness in your partner, and crisis heroics creates learned helplessness in your team. Taking on more than your share of emotional responsibility prevents relationship growth, and absorbing all the crisis management prevents team growth. The over functioning pattern showed me how my 'helpful' interventions were disrupting the leadership work I was trying to do. Every time I rushed in to solve a problem someone else could handle, I built dependence rather than capability. Every time I absorbed someone else's anxiety about a difficult decision, I designed systems that required my constant intervention.

Sound familiar? It should. It's the same dynamic that happens when technical leaders become addicted to being the person who fixes everything.

The over-functioning pattern often emerges from a desperate attempt to feel some control in relationships where your partner isn't carrying their weight, or where there's emotional chaos you're trying to manage. Sometimes it's the result of cultural expectations—particularly for women—to manage the emotional and logistical load while the other person benefits from that effort without reciprocating.

What makes this pattern so insidious is that it feels like love. It feels like leadership. It feels like being responsible and caring and competent. This works until you realize you're enabling someone else's incompetence while slowly suffocating under the weight of responsibilities that should be shared. The same crisis addiction patterns that showed up in my technical leadership appeared everywhere in my personal life:

In parenting: I caught myself getting a small thrill when my kids had problems that only I could solve. When my oldest couldn't find his favorite shirt before school, instead of teaching them to organize their room or plan ahead, I'd swoop in with a solution. When my youngest struggled with a school project, rather than helping them develop problem-solving skills, I'd take over and fix it myself. I raised children who learned to wait for Mom to handle everything instead of growing their own capabilities. I created the very dependency in my family that I recognized as problematic in my work teams.

In friendships: I became the person everyone called during their relationship crises, career meltdowns, or family emergencies. I prided myself on being available, on having good advice, on being the friend who could handle anyone's emotional chaos. What I didn't notice was that these friendships became one-sided. People came to me for support, but

I rarely reached out when I needed the same. I trained my social circle to see me as the crisis manager rather than as someone who might also need support.

In romantic relationships: I found myself attracted to partners with potential. These are people who had great qualities buried under layers of unaddressed issues. I'd enter relationships thinking I could help them become their best selves, that my emotional intelligence and problem-solving skills could guide them toward growth. Instead, I became their personal development manager, taking responsibility for their emotional work while they remained passive participants in their own lives.

The Emotional Reckoning

I agonized over realizing that I was part of the problem I'd been congratulating myself for solving. My identity as a leader was built on being the person who could handle anything. The expert who remained calm under pressure. The problem-solver who found solutions when others couldn't. If I stopped being the crisis hero, who was I?

What made this even more difficult was that my addiction to firefighting was being reinforced by the organizational culture around me. Senior management noticed and praised the dramatic saves. The team appreciated my willingness to jump in when things got chaotic. Customers valued my responsiveness during emergencies. No one rewarded prevention. No one celebrated the disasters that didn't happen.

Breaking free would mean giving up the immediate gratification of being the hero for the long-term satisfaction of being… what? Someone whose contributions were invisible?

The Invisible Victory Problem

Shifting from reactive to proactive leadership required me to change how I derived satisfaction from my work. Instead of the adrenaline rush of solving emergencies, I learned to find meaning in the quiet work of preventing problems that might never become visible. Instead of being the expert with all the answers, I became the person who asked better questions before problems emerged. Instead of recognition for dramatic saves, I found fulfillment in the invisible victories that no one would ever applaud.

This transition was psychologically brutal because prevention work is inherently invisible. When you solve a crisis, people notice. When you prevent one from happening in the first place, nobody even knows there was a problem to solve. When a fire doesn't start, no one celebrates your foresight. When conflicts are resolved before they escalate, no one notices the skill required to navigate those early conversations.

For months, I felt like I wasn't contributing. I went from being the visible hero who saved the day to being the invisible leader whose contributions couldn't be measured. The upstream work of having conversations about potential issues, building better processes, and creating early warning systems felt less important than the urgent technical challenges that kept appearing.

My old identity kept pulling me back toward the fires. When a crisis emerged, every instinct screamed at me to dive in and solve it myself. Resisting that urge felt like abandoning my responsibility as a leader. There were days when I would see other technical leaders getting praise for their dramatic crisis management, and I'd feel jealous. Part of me wanted to go back to the adrenaline and recognition of emergency response.

Gradually, I saw the results of the prevention work. Not dramatic results—quiet results. Problems that didn't appear. Conflicts that didn't escalate. Risks that were caught early enough to address systematically rather than frantically.

The team's stress level decreased. Our work quality improved. We had more time for innovation because we weren't constantly in recovery mode. My team members built their own problem-solving capabilities because they weren't waiting for me to rescue them from every challenge.

The only thing that kept me committed to the upstream approach was watching the long-term impact on my team. They became more confident, more proactive, and more capable of excellent independent work. I learned to get my satisfaction from their growth rather than from external recognition of my own heroics.

The View from Outside:
When Prevention Feels Like Another Task

Here's the part that would be hilarious if it weren't so exhausting: I'm fighting fires and the team says, "You should take some time off, maybe go to the spa, leave early." They're clearly aware I'm struggling to keep up with the load, and their response is for me to rest? In my mind, that adds one more thing to my to-do list. Resting becomes a *task* and not restoration.

This reminds me of Emily and Amelia Nagoski's[11] groundbreaking research in *Burnout: The Secret to Unlocking the Stress Cycle*. The Nagoski sisters make a crucial distinction that shifts how we understand workplace exhaustion: an absence of rest or

---

11 Nagoski, E., & Nagoski, A. (2019). *Burnout: The Secret to Unlocking the Stress Cycle*. Ballantine Books.

a personal failure to manage stress effectively do not cause burn-out. It's a systemic issue that requires addressing the underlying conditions that create chronic stress and not adding self-care activities on top of an already overwhelming workload.

Their research reveals that burnout happens when we get stuck in incomplete stress cycles. This is when our bodies activate stress responses to handle workplace challenges but never get the opportunity to complete those biological cycles through movement, creative expression, emotional processing, or genuine rest. The problem isn't that people aren't trying hard enough to take care of themselves; it's that they're operating in systems that continuously trigger stress responses while providing no realistic opportunities for recovery.

When your team suggests you "take a break," they're unconsciously treating burnout like a personal energy management problem rather than recognizing it as a systemic failure in how work is organized and distributed. The Nagoski sisters emphasize that individual wellness strategies—while personally beneficial—cannot solve burnout that originates from systemic workplace dysfunction.

What made this particularly insidious in my case was that the crisis addiction itself prevented the systemic changes that could have eliminated most of the stress. I was so busy heroically responding to fires that I couldn't step back to see how my own behavior created the conditions that required constant crisis management. The team's well-meaning suggestion to *rest more* reinforced the same pattern. It treated my exhaustion as a personal problem rather than addressing the leadership approach that created unsustainable demands on everyone.

What they couldn't see (and neither could I) wasn't that I needed more downtime. The problem was that I had built an entire professional identity around being indispensable during disasters, and I was actively preventing the upstream thinking that would eliminate most of those disasters in the first place.

The real solution was changing the systems that required constant crisis response. That required other people to understand that prevention work is as important as crisis response, even when it's less visible.

Management had mixed feelings about my eventual shift toward upstream thinking. They appreciated the improved outcomes, but they were nervous about what looked like less direct involvement in immediate problems. They were used to seeing me jump into every crisis. My fresh approach of coaching others through problems felt less… *leaderly* to them. Where was the dramatic problem-solving? Where were the visible heroics they'd come to associate with effective leadership?

My team had to adjust its expectations, too. Some of them had grown comfortable with—even enjoyed—the drama and importance of crisis response. When I stopped jumping in to save them from every challenge, some felt abandoned or unsupported, even though I built their capabilities. They missed the adrenaline rush of emergency mode and the clear sense of purpose that came with fighting fires together.

From their perspective, I was a heroic leader who simply needed better work-life balance. From reality's perspective, I was an exhausted leader who was inadvertently creating the very problems I was killing myself to solve. The suggestions came from a place of genuine care, and they missed the point. You can't spa-day your way out of a dysfunctional system you're actively maintaining.

The Mindset Shift

One pattern particularly caught my attention because it revealed how my firefighting addiction created the very problems I was solving. We kept seeing assembly defects that traced back to the same root cause. Small misalignments, missing fasteners, incorrect torque values—nothing catastrophic, but enough to create rework and delays. My immediate reaction was classic firefighting. *The technicians need to be more careful*; we *need better quality control*; let's *add another inspection step*. I treated the symptoms and felt good about my responsiveness to quality issues.

When we dug deeper, we discovered that our assembly procedures had been written by engineers for experienced technicians. They assumed certain intuitive adjustments that experienced technicians would naturally make. When the newer team members followed the procedures literally, errors emerged.

I'd reviewed those procedures. I'd been so close to the assembly for so long that expecting these nuances came naturally. By failing to think from a new technician's point of view, I spent months heroically solving the problems my haste had created. We weren't facing a technician problem. We were facing a leadership problem. Specifically, a *me* problem.

Instead of adding more inspection layers, we rewrote the procedures with input from the people who used them. We added visual guides, clarified ambiguous steps, and explained the reasoning behind critical sequences. The defect rate plummeted. We didn't catch more errors; we prevented them from happening in the first place.

If I'd taken the time upfront to write procedures properly, I never would have gotten the recognition for solving the quality crisis. I would have been the leader whose procedures worked so well that no one noticed them.

The assembly procedure revelation hit me hard because I remembered Maria's attention to detail and how much better our procedures became when I included her input. I'd gotten lazy by approving procedures without the thorough review that Maria had taught me was essential. My firefighting addiction made me careless about the very upstream work that I knew prevented problems.

My firefighting addiction was literally creating opportunities for me to look good by solving problems I'd helped create. I had built a system where my team depended on my heroic interventions rather than building their own problem-solving capabilities. The work procedures failure sounded technical, but it was actually human.

When It Goes Wrong: The (Not So) Surprising Hospitalization

Ending up in a hospital bed while working on a project designed to send humans safely into space was not the way this story was supposed to go.

It was the aftermath of our most ambitious rocket build yet—a project that had stretched our team, our resources, and apparently my physical limits beyond what any of us had imagined possible. What started as a challenging but manageable timeline had devolved into an eighty-hour-a-week nightmare of emerging problems, parts delays, and resource constraints that seemed to multiply faster than we could solve them.

I'd thrown myself into crisis mode with the intensity I'd learned in my Air Force days. Every problem became my problem. Every delay became my personal mission to overcome. Every frustrated stakeholder became someone I needed to reassure, manage, and somehow satisfy despite increasingly impossible circumstances.

The warning signs had been there for months. The exhaustion that coffee couldn't touch. The way my heart would race during routine meetings. The strange aches and pains that I kept pushing through because there was always another fire to fight. The autoimmune symptoms that I attributed to stress and kept treating with over-the-counter solutions because I didn't have time for doctor visits. Until my body decided for me. I had chest pain. My pulse raced. My vision closed in. All the classic heart symptoms that are supposed to send you to the Emergency Room.

Sitting in that hospital bed, connected to monitors and waiting for test results that would take months to interpret, I had plenty of time to think about how I'd gotten there. The doctors couldn't pinpoint exactly what had triggered the cascade of symptoms—chronic stress, autoimmune flare-up, burnout manifesting as physical breakdown. What they could tell me was that my body had essentially gone on strike against the unsustainable pace I'd been maintaining.

The wake-up call shocked me. It was my system—both physical and professional—demanding that I finally learn the difference between crisis response and crisis creation. The hospitalization was my body's way of forcing me to confront what I'd been unwilling to address: that my crisis addiction was literally making me sick.

Chronic over-functioning creates measurable physiological changes. Research has established clear connections between stress and autoimmune disease development. According to Harvard Health, "persistent stress (such as worry about finances, mental or physical health, or interpersonal relationships) could lead to chronic diseases such as high blood pressure or autoimmune disease"[12].

---

12 Harvard Health Publishing. (2018). Autoimmune disease and stress: Is there a link? Harvard Medical School. https://www.health.harvard.edu/blog/autoimmune-disease-and-stress-is-there-a-link-201807114230

Your nervous system gets stuck in fight-or-flight mode. Your immune system becomes hypervigilant. Your adrenal glands burn out from constantly producing stress hormones. A major study published in the Journal of the American Medical Association found that individuals diagnosed with stress-related disorders were more likely to develop autoimmune diseases compared to those without such disorders.[13]

The medical professionals I worked with helped me understand that autoimmune conditions often develop in people who've spent years managing everyone else's problems while neglecting their own needs. Studies indicate that up to 80% of patients with autoimmune conditions report experiencing significant emotional stress before disease onset.[14] The body eventually rebels against the unsustainable pattern when chronic stress disrupts immune function and leads to increased systemic inflammation.

My recovery required more than simple rest. It required completely restructuring my approach to work and relationships. I had to learn to set boundaries, delegate effectively, and resist the urge to jump into every crisis. More importantly, I had to accept that my value as a leader didn't depend on being indispensable during emergencies. In fact, my addiction to crisis management made me less effective as a leader because it prevented me from building sustainable systems. My hospitalization became a turning point that forced me to choose between short-term heroics and long-term effectiveness.

---

13 Song, H., Fang, F., Tomasson, G., et al. (2018). Association of stress-related disorders with subsequent autoimmune disease. *JAMA*, 319(23), 2388-2400.

14 Global Autoimmune Institute. (2024). Stress & autoimmune disease: Navigating the complex relationship. https://www.autoimmuneinstitute.org/articles/stress-autoimmune-disease-navigating-the-complex-relationship/

The Recovery System:
Learning to Find Satisfaction
in What Doesn't Happen

Two weeks after my big revelation about fire-fighting addiction, a major integration issue emerged, and I dove in to solve it personally, like in the old days. I was three hours into debugging the problem when Sarah walked by my office. "Thought you were focusing on upstream work now," she said with a knowing smile.

She reminded me that recovery from crisis addiction requires the same vigilance as any other addiction. I had to learn to recognize the triggers—the adrenaline surge when problems emerged, the satisfaction of being needed, the fear that others couldn't handle the complexity. I created a personal protocol. When I felt the urge to jump into crisis mode, I paused and asked whether this was something only I could solve, or an opportunity for someone else to grow? More often than not, it was the latter.

The hardest part was learning to find satisfaction in other people's victories instead of my own. In this shift, I had to learn to get satisfaction from:

- **Meetings that ended early** because we'd addressed potential issues before they became urgent problems.
- **Projects that stayed on schedule** because we'd identified and mitigated risks during planning rather than discovering them during execution.
- **Teams that worked smoothly** because we'd invested in communication and process improvement rather than relying on crisis management to force collaboration.
- **Stakeholder relationships remained positive** because we'd addressed concerns proactively rather than reactively.

Engineering work that focused on innovation because we weren't constantly putting out fires.

None of these outcomes generated the adrenaline rush or external recognition of crisis heroics. They were infinitely more valuable for long-term mission success.

Learning to appreciate quiet victories required me to create a completely different relationship with work satisfaction. Instead of getting validation from being needed during emergencies, I had to find meaning in creating conditions where emergencies were rare.

The FFMEA Mindset Shift

One tool that helped me transition from reactive to proactive thinking was adopting the Functional Failure Mode and Effects Analysis (FFMEA[15]) mindset. I didn't use this as a formal document, but as a way of thinking about everything we did.

Regular FFMEA thinking means asking, "What could go wrong, and how would we know early enough to prevent it?"

During a recent hardware move at Kennedy Space Center, our team conducted an informal FFMEA that considered everything from equipment failures to environmental conditions. Someone asked, "What if it rains during transport?" My old self would have dismissed that as overthinking. The weather forecast was clear. We had contingency plans if things got delayed. Why worry about unlikely scenarios?

The new, upstream-thinking version of me recognized this as exactly the question that prevents disasters. That simple "what if"

---

15 Burge, Stuart. "The Systems Engineering Toolbox." *Burge Hughes Walsh*, 2010, www.burgehugheswalsh.co.uk/Uploaded/1/Documents/FFMEA-Tool-v1-2.pdf.

led us to revise our procedures and staging areas. When unexpected storms hit during the operation, we were prepared.

The power of FFMEA thinking isn't in the documentation. It's in building a culture where everyone feels safe questioning assumptions and anticipating failures. This requires building an emotional infrastructure where raising concerns is rewarded rather than dismissed, where uncertainty is explored rather than hidden. It's building the habit of identifying potential risks, even when systems appear to be performing well.

Adopting this mindset required me to give up the excitement of improvising solutions under pressure. Prevention is more boring and much more effective than crisis response.

The Team Impact of My Transformation

I was surprised to see how my shift from firefighting to prevention would affect my team's growth. When I was the crisis hero, my team learned to depend on me for solutions. They would encounter problems and wait for me to fix them. They developed learned helplessness because they knew I would eventually step in and handle whatever was going wrong.

When I focused on upstream prevention, something remarkable happened: they solved problems themselves. This didn't happen automatically because I stepped back. I had to intentionally architect new systems that made their independence feel safer than their dependence on me.

Instead of jumping in with solutions when they brought me problems, I tried different conversations: "What do you think is causing this?" and "What approaches have you considered?" I designed a space for them to think through problems before offering my input.

I created new reward systems that celebrated their problem-solving rather than my problem-solving. When Maria caught a quality issue early, I made sure to recognize her upstream thinking in team meetings. When Eric prevented an integration problem through better planning, I highlighted how his proactive approach saved the program time and resources.

I had to build psychological safety around their mistakes and learning. Instead of treating their struggles as inefficiencies I needed to fix, I framed their challenges as capability building that served our long-term mission success.

Designing new systems where they couldn't default to me was the solution this team needed. This was about rebuilding the emotional infrastructure so that taking initiative felt safer than waiting for rescue. Because I asked better questions upfront, they learned to anticipate and address issues before they became crises.

Maria caught potential quality issues during design reviews instead of waiting for them to show up during assembly. Eric identified integration challenges during planning rather than discovering them during hardware installation. Tom raised concerns about schedule risks before they became schedule crises. They were becoming upstream thinkers themselves.

This transformation required me to resist every instinct to jump in and solve their problems for them. I had to watch them struggle with challenges I could have fixed quickly, knowing that their struggle was building capability I could never give them by solving problems on their behalf.

Coaching Conversations:
Questions for Recognizing Crisis Addiction

When I coach technical professionals about crisis addiction, I use a series of questions to help them recognize their own patterns:

"When do you feel most valuable in your professional role? During smooth operations or during emergencies?"

Most crisis-driven professionals will admit that they feel more important when things are going wrong and they can step in to fix them.

"What problems keep recurring in your organization that you're good at solving?"

This question often reveals the cycles where technical teams are unconsciously creating the problems they're heroically solving.

"How often do you think it won't get done right if you don't do it?"

This belief is usually a sign that the individual hasn't invested in building collective capabilities because they're too busy being the hero.

"What would happen to your team if you were unavailable for a month?"

Crisis-addicted leaders often realize that their teams would struggle because they've never been required to learn independent problem-solving skills.

The key is helping people recognize that while crisis addiction feels like good leadership, it constrains organizational capability. You can't build resilient teams if you're constantly rescuing them from challenges they should learn to handle themselves.

Reflection Framework:
Assessing Your Crisis Addiction

Pattern Recognition: Are You Creating the Problems You're Solving?

Crisis addiction is seductive because it feels like you're doing a great job. The key is recognizing when your "heroic" problem-solving is preventing your team from developing their own capabilities.

Look at Your Last Month

What problems keep recurring that you've become good at solving? If you're seeing the same issues across different projects, you might be addressing symptoms rather than root causes.

When do you feel most valuable and energized as a leader? If it's during emergencies rather than smooth operations, that's a warning sign that you need crises to feel important.

How often do you think *it won't get done right if I don't do it?* This belief usually indicates you haven't invested time in developing others' capabilities because you're too busy being the hero.

What skills are your team members not learning because you consistently handle certain types of problems? If people always bring you their challenges instead of their proposed solutions, you're creating dependency rather than capability.

One Thing to Try This Week

The next time a recurring problem emerges, stop solving it immediately. Instead, ask, "This is the third time we've seen this issue. What's happening upstream that's allowing this pattern to continue?" Focus on fixing the system that creates the problem rather than fixing the problem itself.

Playbook:
Transitioning from Crisis
Response to Crisis Prevention

When You Notice Recurring Problem Patterns

If you keep seeing similar problems emerge across different projects, and you're getting good at solving them quickly, this is a sign you need to intervene.

Watch for teams addicted to the recognition that comes from heroic problem-solving, root causes above your level to address, or prevention work that feels less urgent than current crises.

Stop solving immediately and start investigating: "Where is our process breaking down that's allowing this problem to repeat?"

Gather your team for root cause analysis: "Instead of fixing this again, let's figure out how to prevent it from happening."

Look for systemic issues: "What assumptions, processes, or communication gaps are allowing this problem to persist?"

Invest in prevention: "What would we need to change upfront to make this problem impossible?"

Recurring challenges almost always point to a systemic concern that needs attention. Looking at your process is likely to show you where you can change and reduce the number of times you solve the same issue.

When Your Team Waits for Rescue

Is your team consistently bringing you problems to solve rather than coming up with proposed solutions?

Watch for team members who lack confidence in their problem-solving abilities, previous managers who trained them to escalate issues, or problems that genuinely are above their skill level.

Change your response pattern: "What solutions have you considered?" before diving into problem-solving mode.

Create mentoring opportunities: "This is a great chance for you to practice your troubleshooting skills. What's your approach?"

Resist the urge to rescue: "I'm confident you can figure this out. Let me know what you discover."

Celebrate independent problem-solving: "I love that you solved this with no need to escalate it."

This could be a training issue. Sometimes leaders inadvertently create an environment where bringing a solution feels dangerous. So, check your own behavior and see how you might be making it uncomfortable for your team to bring you solutions. This could also be a sign that your team is over their heads and needs to tap into other resources to explore potential options. Lots of curiosity is important here.

When You're Addicted to Crisis Drama

Use this section when you realize you're drawn to dramatic problem-solving and struggle to find satisfaction in steady-state operations.

Watch for addiction patterns too strong to change without external support, roles that genuinely require crisis management, or organizations that only reward crisis heroics.

Recognize the addiction pattern: "I'm getting excited about problems I should be preventing."

Retrain your reward system: "What quiet victories happened this week that nobody noticed?"

Find appropriate challenges: "Where can I apply my crisis management skills to prevent future crises?"

Build others' crisis capabilities: "How can I teach someone else to handle emergencies so I can focus on prevention?"

It's hard to let go of your own need to feel important and desire to solve your team's problems. While you can work through this on your own, getting insight from a coach, therapist, or mentor speeds this along.

When Crisis Management Is Over-functioning

Sometimes, you realize that much of your 'crisis management' is over-functioning. This shows up as managing other people's anxiety about predictable problems instead of helping them build their own capability to handle challenges.

Watch for people unconsciously dumping emotional labor, emotional crises masking real technical problems, or boundaries around emotional work that need strengthening.

Distinguish technical crises from anxiety dumps: "Is this an actual emergency, or is someone asking me to manage their anxiety about a normal challenge?"

Address the upstream over-functioning patterns: "What would help people feel more confident handling this type of situation independently?"

Build emotional capability in others: "How can we distribute the emotional work of problem-solving instead of concentrating it on me?"

Create emotional early warning systems: "What are the signs that someone is about to dump their crisis anxiety on me?"

Much like in the last scenario, over-functioning can be difficult to shift because it's something you've learned to succeed in a technical environment. It served you well in that time, and it's time to develop a new focus. Now you look at setting your team up for success, not carrying them with your own effort.

The Long Game Advantage

Looking back, I can see the compound benefits of breaking my firefighting addiction, though the results weren't always as permanent or transformative as I'd hoped. When I shifted from crisis response to prevention thinking, the immediate improvements were dramatic.

- My team became more capable of independent problem-solving because they weren't waiting for me to rescue them from every challenge. The team that was *difficult* thought more proactively.
- Stakeholder trust increased as our reliability improved and surprises became rare. Management gave us more latitude to make independent decisions.
- Innovation became possible when we weren't constantly in crisis-recovery mode. This gave us room to build systems to enable sustainable performance.
- My stress decreased significantly as crisis mode became the exception rather than the norm. I had time to focus on my health, to build resilience, and to reflect on where I wanted to go next.
- Quality improved as systems prevented errors instead of catching them. We had more time to work on the next challenges instead of fixing the errors.
- I created capacity for the work that mattered, which moved missions forward. I no longer felt I was running to keep up.

Some changes stick, and some changes require ongoing reinforcement. The systemic improvements—better processes, clearer communication patterns, more reliable delivery—those changes had staying power because they were built into how we worked together. The individual development gains were more variable.

Some people embraced the increased responsibility and continued to grow. Others reverted to their baseline patterns when the external pressure for change diminished.

This taught me something important about the difference between enabling temporary performance improvements and creating lasting capability growth. I could create conditions where people performed at higher levels, but I couldn't force them to internalize those higher standards permanently. Some growth requires the individual to choose it repeatedly.

The prevention work still paid dividends long after my direct involvement ended. The processes, the upstream thinking, the systems we'd built to catch problems early—those continued to function. The human element? That required more ongoing attention than I'd anticipated.

Specific Crisis Prevention Techniques

Shifting into a focus on prevention rather than crisis can feel overwhelming and leave you searching for where to start. There are so many different parts of a technical leader's job that would benefit from this kind of shift. I've listed a few small ways you can carefully tread into this ocean. Some of these are simple, and you can start today. Others may need a little pre-planning.

Weekly Pattern Analysis: Every Friday, spend 30 minutes reviewing the week's "urgent" issues. Ask: "What upstream decision could have prevented this?" Track patterns over time.

Early Warning Systems: Identify the leading indicators for your most common crises. Create checkpoints that catch problems when they're still manageable rather than when they've become emergencies.

Decision Pre-mortems: Before major decisions, ask, "If this goes wrong in six months, what will the failure mode look like?" Design prevention into the decision rather than planning for a heroic response.

Capability Building: For each crisis you handle personally, ask, "How could I have equipped someone else to handle this?" Create development opportunities around your most frequent firefighting activities.

Stakeholder Expectation Management: Stop rewarding crisis response with praise and recognition. Start celebrating prevention and early problem-solving even when it's less visible.

The Ongoing Recovery

Even now, I still feel the pull of crisis heroics. When a technical emergency arises, part of me wants to dive in personally and save the day. The adrenaline is still appealing. The recognition is still gratifying. I've learned to recognize that impulse and choose consciously whether to act on it.

Sometimes, the situation genuinely requires my personal intervention. More often, jumping in would deprive someone else of a growth opportunity while reinforcing my addiction to being indispensable.

Recovery from firefighting addiction is about creating new organizational systems, not simply changing personal habits. Design reward systems that celebrate prevention, create processes that enable proactive thinking, and build cultural infrastructure where heroes aren't needed.

I discovered my crisis addiction was connected to another pattern I hadn't recognized: my addiction to being needed. The same impulse that made me rush toward every emergency also made me reluctant to let others handle important work. I said I wanted to mentor my team, but I kept finding reasons why I should handle the critical conversations, make the difficult decisions, and manage the stakeholder relationships myself.

I substituted one form of indispensability for another. Instead of being the crisis hero, I became the capability bottleneck. Both patterns served the same underlying need: feeling essential. Both patterns prevented my team from learning the independence they needed to excel. I had to learn to break free from the need to be needed.

The most important realization I made is that problems that feel like they need a hero usually need better systems. When you stop being the hero, you can start building the conditions where heroes aren't needed.

In the next chapter, we'll explore how this upstream mindset enables one of the most important aspects of technical leadership: mentoring other leaders who can carry this preventive approach forward, building organizations that create excellence rather than responding to crises.

Building Leaders, Not Dependencies

Chapter 8

Years into my chief engineer role, with frameworks for conflict and crisis management well-established, I faced my next major leadership challenge, building the next generation of leaders to eventually take my job.

Sitting in the conference room, looking at the agenda for what was shaping up to be a contentious discussion about a fluids system issue, I craved stepping in to handle it personally. The customer pushed for additional testing, more analysis, and component swaps that our team believed were unnecessary. There were difficult feelings on all sides. Program management was nervous. Company management would be watching.

This was exactly the high-stakes technical conversation I'd been managing for years. The kind where reputations get made or broken. The kind where one wrong word can derail months of work. Across the table sat Tyler, one of the emerging engineers in our program's Technical Leadership Development Program. Tyler understood the system deeply, had done excellent work on the analysis, and possessed the technical credibility to represent our position effectively.

Tyler had also never presented to this level of stakeholder audience before. Never navigated the political complexity of customer pushback. Never had to communicate complex technical concepts to people whose expertise lay in program management, not fluid dynamics.

I could solve this problem. Or I could build Tyler's capacity to solve the next ten problems like it. This was about the fundamental choice between building organizational dependence and building organizational capability. Every time I stepped in to handle what someone else could learn to handle, I was building systems that required my intervention rather than systems that could function independently. The choice felt obvious in principle. In practice, it required every ounce of self-discipline I possessed not to upset the team dynamics I was trying to build.

Here's what was screaming in my head: *What if Tyler screws this up? What if he can't handle the pressure? What if the customer loses confidence in our technical capability? What if this damages relationships I've spent years building? What if I look like an irresponsible leader for putting someone inexperienced in such a critical situation?*

Underneath all those rational concerns was the deeper, more uncomfortable truth that said I didn't want to let go. I liked being the person who handled the difficult conversations. I was good at it. It made me feel important, needed, indispensable. Mentoring Tyler meant accepting that I wasn't the only one who could do this work. That felt like losing something fundamental about my identity as a leader.

Origin Story:
The Lifelong Mission to Enable Potential

My passion for mentoring others started early, though I didn't recognize it as leadership training at the time. I was nine years old, standing in front of my fourth-grade class, practically vibrating with excitement as I talked about the Apollo moon landings and the upcoming space shuttle program. My teacher had asked us to share something we were passionate about, and I'd prepared a ten-minute presentation on why human spaceflight was the most amazing thing happening in our world.

I wanted everyone in that classroom to feel what I felt when I watched those grainy Apollo footage clips years before. I wanted them to understand that we were living through an extraordinary time, when humans were preparing to make space travel more routine with this new shuttle they were developing and testing. I wanted to share the excitement of what was coming next in space exploration.

Did I convert any of my classmates to careers in aerospace? Probably not, but I did learn that I got as much satisfaction from sharing knowledge as I did from acquiring it. Maybe more. That pattern followed me to college where I tutored struggling engineering students because I loved watching someone's face change when a difficult concept finally clicked. In my early career, I sought mentoring opportunities with new engineers. As I advanced, I found myself drawn to coaching emerging leaders.

There was a line from Star Trek that captured what I was trying to do. It has stayed with me for years, and in the context of this book, it became even more impactful. In *Star Trek: Nemesis,* Captain Picard tells his clone, "Buried deep within you, beneath all the years of pain and anger, there is something that has never been nurtured: the potential to make yourself a better man. That is what it is to be human. To make yourself more than you are."

That quote became a core value for how I approached leadership: the belief that every person has untapped potential that can be unlocked under the right conditions. It also revealed something about my own psychological makeup that would later create challenges—I was drawn to the role of the person who could see and nurture that potential in others.

From fourth grade onward, I naturally gravitated toward teaching and mentoring roles. There was something else embedded in that pattern that I didn't recognize until much later: I was also drawn to people who needed mentoring and growth. I felt most valuable when I was helping someone become better than they currently were. This created a subtle and important (and not always positive) bias in my leadership approach that would take years to recognize and address.

The Mentor's Dilemma

I thought mentoring Tyler would feel like teaching. I shared what I knew with someone eager to learn. I didn't think it would feel like losing pieces of my identity. Every technique I taught Tyler, every insight I shared, every approach I explained meant he'd eventually be able to handle conversations that used to require me personally. Part of me celebrated his growth. Another part of me wondered what would happen to my value as a leader if people didn't need me to solve their problems anymore.

When you're an individual contributor, your value comes from your personal technical excellence. You solve problems, you deliver results, you demonstrate expertise. Success is measurable and immediate, directly tied to your own capabilities. When you become a technical leader, your value should come from multiplying technical excellence across your entire team. Success becomes indirect and delayed, dependent on other people's growth.

Making that transition requires fighting against every instinct that made you successful as an engineer:

The desire to personally solve complex problems because you know you can do it well. Why spend three hours coaching someone through a solution when you could implement it yourself in thirty minutes? The math seems obvious until you realize you're creating dependency instead of capability.

The satisfaction of being the expert everyone turns to because it feels like validation of your competence. There's an addictive quality to being the person with the answers, the one who can untangle the most complex technical challenges. Stepping back from that role can feel like losing your identity.

The fear that others won't do it as well as you would because your standards are high and you care about outcomes. What if they make mistakes you would have avoided? What if their approach is less elegant, less efficient, less perfect than what you would have done?

The impatience with the messiness of mentoring versus the cleanliness of doing it yourself. Mentoring is slow and full of setbacks. It requires allowing people to struggle, to fail, to learn through experience rather than instruction. It requires tolerating inefficiency in service of long-term capability building.

The addiction to being needed, because being indispensable feels like job security. If you're the only one who can handle the critical problems, you'll always have a role. If you show others how to handle those problems, what happens to your unique value?

Every one of these instincts tells you to take over rather than teach. To solve rather than build. To maintain control rather than share ownership. They're not wrong instincts. They served you well as an individual contributor. They become liabilities when your job shifts from doing the work to enabling others to do the work.

The hardest part of becoming a great technical leader is learning to get your satisfaction from other people's growth rather than your own performance. It requires rewiring your reward system, redefining what success looks like, and finding new sources of professional fulfillment. I fought that transition every step of the way.

I Didn't Want to Mentor Others

I have struggled for years to admit that part of me didn't want other people to become as capable as I was. I wasn't being malicious. I didn't want to sabotage anyone's career or hoard opportunities. I felt important when complex problems required my personal attention. Feeling irreplaceable was enjoyable.

Mentoring others meant potentially making myself less central to the team's success. It meant accepting that Tyler might eventually handle customer relationships as well as I did, or that Maria might become better at risk assessment than I was, or that Eric might learn design insights that surpassed my own. That felt threatening, even though I knew intellectually that it was exactly what good leadership required.

My inner voice had few good things to say: *Was I committed to the mission's success, or was I committed to my own importance? Was I building a sustainable organization, or was I building my own indispensability?* The answers were uncomfortable because they revealed how much of my work had been about serving my own psychological needs rather than mentoring others' capabilities.

How This Shows Up Everywhere: Learning to Let Go When You Don't Want To

The lessons about building leaders instead of dependencies hit closest to home when they played out in my family. The summer my youngest graduated high school, both of my kids embarked on extended trips on their own—the kind of adventures that would have been unthinkable when they were younger and that felt like necessary steps toward independence now that they were approaching adulthood.

My oldest planned two cross-country trips to see concerts by a favorite band. My youngest organized a multi-week National Park tour that would take them across the western U.S. and Canada. As their departure dates approached, I cycled through the same emotions I experienced when mentoring team members: excitement about their growth, pride in their capability, and an uncomfortable undercurrent of anxiety about letting go of control.

It was challenging to trust that they had thought of all the things they might need. I caught myself wanting to review their itineraries in detail, to offer suggestions about packing, to make sure they had contingency plans for every possible scenario. The same perfectionist tendencies that made me want to solve problems for my team were now making me want to over-manage my children's adventures.

I eagerly awaited their text confirmations that they were safe and making good decisions. When those messages were delayed or brief, I resisted the urge to text multiple follow-up questions.

Their trips weren't perfect. There were missed connections, weather delays, personality conflicts with travel companions, and disappointments about activities that didn't work out as expected.

When they returned home—tired, a bit frustrated with some aspects of their trips, but overall doing well—I realized we had all learned important lessons. They learned about the way they show up for their friends, how to ask others for help when they need it, and how to adapt when circumstances don't match expectations. I learned how to let them go and trust that the things I'd taught them over the years would serve them well as they took their first real steps into independent adulthood.

The same control addiction that constrained my technical leadership showed up everywhere in my personal life: the urge to solve rather than teach, to prevent struggle rather than allow growth, to maintain oversight rather than trust capability. Learning to become a mentor rather than a problem solver required rewiring my reward system in every relationship, not just my professional ones.

The Fear That Never Goes Away

Even when I committed to mentoring Tyler for that customer presentation, the fear was overwhelming. These fears weren't irrational. They were legitimate concerns about real risks. Mentoring others creates short-term vulnerability. There is a chance that someone learning will make mistakes you wouldn't make. I learned that avoiding those risks meant creating a larger risk: building an organization that couldn't function without me. In this (and really every) situation, I needed to shift to choosing between short-term risk for long-term capability versus short-term safety for long-term fragility.

The fear becomes particularly acute when you realize that successful mentoring means your role will change. As Tyler becomes more capable, I'm no longer the person who handles every customer relationship or consults on every technical approach. This transition requires grieving the loss of your previous identity as the indispensable expert while embracing a new identity as someone who builds capability in others. The fear is about who I am when I'm no longer the person everyone needs for everything.

You can't architect independence if the lead designer is terrified of becoming obsolete. My fingerprints were all over the team's dysfunction. My anger created a chilling effect on innovation, and my bargaining for control turned what should have been an open system into a closed loop. I was so busy trying to be the essential piece of the puzzle that I forgot my real job was to build a picture that didn't need me at all.

I had to design my own emotional recovery before I could effectively nurture others' growth. The two processes weren't separate. They were the same work at different scales. I was surprised at how this personal emotional journey directly impacted the organizational emotional architecture I tried to build. When I operated from fear about being replaced, I unconsciously sabotaged the very development opportunities I tried to create. When I was stuck in anger at others' imperfections, I created emotional environments where people felt unsafe to take risks. When I bargained to maintain control, I designed systems that kept people dependent rather than enabling independence.

Tyler's Coaching Conversation

Instead of preparing my own presentation for the customer meeting, I coached Tyler on how to approach the conversation. That coaching required me to articulate insights and strategies I'd been using intuitively for years.

I taught Tyler how to acknowledge customer concerns without accepting their conclusions outright. We worked through ways to present technical data in language that non-experts could understand, transforming complex analyses into accessible insights. I showed him how to build bridges rather than walls when stakeholders have different risk appetites, navigating the delicate balance between technical accuracy and organizational harmony. Most challenging of all, I had to demonstrate how to maintain confidence in our analysis while showing genuine respect for their perspective.

Sharing this knowledge felt vulnerable because it meant giving up the hard-won wisdom from years of difficult conversations. These approaches were part of what made me valuable as a leader. Every technique I shared, every approach I explained, represented moments when I'd succeeded or failed in high-stakes situations. This was my accumulated experience of navigating complex human dynamics while delivering technical results.

Teaching them to Tyler meant he'd eventually be able to handle these challenging stakeholder interactions independently. The thought was unsettling. If Tyler could execute these conversations using the framework I'd given him, what would that mean for my role? Would I become less essential to the team's success?

Unexpectedly, our preparation for the presentation and my having to articulate my approach to someone else forced me to examine it more systematically. Teaching required me to make explicit the decision-making processes I'd been using unconsciously. I discovered patterns in my thinking that I'd never formally documented, approaches that had become so automatic I'd forgotten they were deliberate choices.

Tyler's questions during our coaching sessions helped me clarify my framework. When he asked, "How do you decide when to push back versus when to accommodate?" I had to think through the criteria I'd been applying intuitively. When he asked, "What signals tell you a stakeholder is genuinely concerned versus posturing?" I had to articulate the pattern recognition I'd developed over years.

The coaching conversation was teaching Tyler how to apply the framework, and it helped me codify what I'd been doing instinctively. His questions weren't revealing flaws in my approach; they were forcing me to document the expertise I'd built so it could be transferred systematically.

I saw that mentoring others didn't diminish my value. It proved my expertise was robust enough to be teachable. The success of the framework was because of its solid principles, not my charisma, and others who learned these principles could apply them effectively.

Tyler's success would be evidence that I'd built something real—a systematic approach to stakeholder management that worked when executed correctly, not magic that only I could perform.

Presentation Day

When the day came, Tyler stepped into that room carrying both his technical expertise and the framework I'd given him for navigating stakeholder complexity.

I sat in the back, watching my architecture in action. Tyler began exactly as we'd practiced: acknowledging the customer's concerns and explaining why those concerns made perfect sense from their perspective. I watched Tyler present using the approach I'd taught him—the same one I'd used successfully for years.

Then, he walked through our analysis using the collaborative exploration framework we'd worked on together. Not "Here's why you're wrong," but "Here's what we're seeing, and here's how we can address your concerns together."

I'd shown him this technique. I'd shown it in similar meetings. I'd coached him through the specific language that transforms adversarial negotiations into collaborative problem-solving. Watching him execute it effectively validated everything I'd built. The customer still pushed for additional assurance, but they were now working with us rather than against us—exactly the outcome this approach achieved.

Tyler had applied the framework correctly under pressure. He'd trusted the architecture I'd given him and executed it without freezing or reverting to defensive posturing. That took courage and skill, and it proved the system worked when someone committed to using it.

By the end of the meeting, Tyler had accomplished exactly what we'd prepared for: he'd defended our technical position while maintaining stakeholder relationships. He'd shown that our technical group could handle complex dynamics because I'd taught people how to do it.

Tyler had built the confidence to handle the next challenge using the same framework—with no need for me to step in and do it for him. Watching the framework succeed through someone else's execution felt better than any personal victory I'd experienced as a leader.

The View from Outside: What Others Were Thinking

As I watched Tyler succeed and I struggled with my own challenging feelings, I realized mentoring opportunities create complex emotional landscapes for everyone involved.

From Tyler's perspective, being asked to handle such a high-stakes conversation was both exciting and terrifying. He told me later that he could see I trusted him with something important, and he also felt the weight of potentially disappointing me or damaging the relationships I'd spent years building. The preparation phase was intense because he knew this was about proving he could represent our team's capabilities at a senior level.

From the customer's perspective, they initially seemed concerned about working with someone less experienced than me. They'd grown accustomed to my approach and weren't sure what to expect. What they experienced was the same collaborative framework I'd been using with them for years, executed by someone who'd been thoroughly coached in how to apply it. One of them mentioned later that they appreciated Tyler's careful preparation and his willingness to ask clarifying questions—both techniques I'd specifically taught him for managing stakeholder concerns. The approach worked because it was sound. Tyler's execution showed that the framework was teachable and repeatable, not dependent on my personal charisma or years of relationship history.

From program management's perspective, they were nervous about having a less senior person represent our technical position in such a critical conversation. Watching Tyler handle the complexity skillfully gave them confidence that our technical organization had depth beyond my individual capabilities. My manager later told me that seeing Tyler succeed made him more comfortable with the idea of me taking on additional responsibilities, knowing the team could function at a high level without my constant oversight.

From my manager's perspective, they were pleased to see emerging leaders taking on more responsibility. After the briefing, they told me, "We never get upset when people bring others up a level. That's exactly what we want to see."

The most interesting insight came from other team members who watched the whole process unfold. Some were inspired by

Tyler's success and asked about taking on similar challenges. Others felt anxious about when they might be asked to step up in comparable ways. A few seemed relieved that the pressure was on someone else. I hadn't expected how much the mentoring process would affect the entire team dynamic.

When Mentoring Goes Wrong: The Unwilling Participant

Not everyone I tried to mentor was ready or willing to grow. I experienced this with someone I'll call Alex, who had strong technical skills and had expressed an interest in evolving beyond his current role, but showed absolutely no interest in doing the work needed to grow.

Alex was technically competent, maybe even brilliant. He could solve complex engineering problems with elegance and efficiency. He understood our systems better than people who had been working on them for years. When given a clear technical task with defined parameters, he delivered excellent results. That's where his engagement ended.

I spent months trying to mentor Alex's leadership capabilities, creating stretch assignments, providing coaching, and offering opportunities to take on more responsibility. Every attempt was met with resistance, deflection, or the half-hearted effort that makes you wonder if you're asking someone to perform surgery while wearing oven mitts.

Carol Dweck's[16] research in *Mindset* helped me understand what happened with Alex. Her studies reveal people fall into

---

16 Dweck, C. S. (2006). *Mindset: The New Psychology of Success*. Random House.

two categories: those with a *growth mindset*, who believe abilities can be built through effort and learning, and those with *a fixed mindset*, who believe talents are static traits. The crucial insight here is that you cannot give someone a growth mindset simply by believing in their potential.

Alex operated with a fixed mindset about his own capabilities. He saw challenges as threats to his competence rather than opportunities to evolve it. When I offered stretch assignments, he experienced them as judgments about his current inadequacy rather than investments in his future capability. My attempts to mentor him felt like criticism of who he was rather than support for who he could become.

Dweck's research shows that a growth mindset must be internally motivated. It comes from the individual's own beliefs about their capacity to learn and improve. I could create conditions that supported a growth mindset, but I couldn't manufacture it in someone who wasn't ready to embrace the discomfort of learning.

I'd assign him to lead a cross-functional review, and he'd execute it like he was reading from a script. The review was technically correct and completely devoid of the relationship-building that makes such meetings effective. I'd offer coaching sessions, and he'd attend and implement exactly none of the suggestions we discussed. I'd create opportunities for him to mentor newer engineers, and he'd defer every difficult conversation back to me. The pattern was consistent: Alex would accept growth opportunities and execute them at the absolute minimum level required to avoid being accused of noncompliance.

I slowly, painfully realized that Alex had no desire to grow into leadership. He was genuinely comfortable in his current role and saw my mentoring efforts as unwanted pressure to become something he didn't want to be. I'd been trying to force someone to value what I valued, to want what I wanted, to see career progression the way I saw it. I projected my own aspirations onto someone who had completely different goals and preferences.

Alex didn't want to manage people, navigate organizational politics, or carry the emotional labor that comes with leadership responsibility. He wanted to solve interesting technical problems within clearly defined boundaries and go home at the end of the day without thinking about work drama. There's nothing wrong with that career choice. What was wrong was my assumption that everyone should want to grow beyond their current role.

This experience taught me that mentoring requires a genuine partnership. You can create opportunities and provide support, but you absolutely cannot force someone to grow. The most effective mentoring happens when someone is actively seeking to expand their capabilities, when they're pulling their growth toward themselves rather than having it pushed onto them.

Now I ask explicitly at the beginning of any potential mentoring relationship, "What kind of growth are you interested in?" followed by, "How can I support your personal growth goals?" rather than assuming everyone wants to follow a leadership path.

Some people want to become technical experts. Others want to build project management skills. Some are interested in customer-facing roles, while others prefer to stay deep in the engineering work. My job as a leader is to support their actual goals, not convert them to mine.

Alex taught me the difference between mentoring people and trying to redesign them. One works. The other is exhausting for everyone involved.

The Multiplication Effect

About three months after Tyler's presentation, he came to my office and said, "I want to set up a mentoring program for the junior engineers. I want to use the approach you used with me."

That moment crystallized what a leadership legacy means. I hadn't just developed one person's capabilities—I'd taught someone how to mentor others using the same architecture.

Over the following months, I watched Tyler apply the framework I'd given him:

- Leading cross-functional teams through technical reviews using the stakeholder management approaches I'd taught
- Mentoring newer engineers with the same preparation and coaching structure I'd used with him
- Representing our technical positions in program discussions using the collaborative problem-solving techniques we'd practiced
- Developing training materials that codified the systems thinking I'd been teaching informally

Each success showed that my framework was repeatable. Tyler had taken the leadership development architecture I'd designed and was now implementing it with other emerging engineers. He was using my coaching techniques, my preparation frameworks, my approaches to building psychological safety.

"The thing is," Tyler explained, "when you mentored me, you taught me how to see potential in others and how to build their capacity systematically. Now I'm using the same process with the team."

That's when I understood what multiplication looked like. Tyler went beyond simple improvements to scaling my framework. The framework I'd developed was now reaching people I didn't have time to mentor personally. The architecture worked exactly as designed: creating leaders who could apply the system to develop more leaders.

Watching Your Framework Succeed Without You

Two years after that customer presentation, Tyler got promoted to lead his own program. When I heard the news, my first reaction surprised me. Along with the pride I expected to feel, there was a tiny stab of something that felt like…jealousy? Tyler hadn't surpassed me. He applied the framework I'd taught him to increasingly complex situations, which was exactly what the architecture enabled. The jealousy was about something more primitive. Tyler was recognized for successfully executing the approach I had developed. He was celebrated for the skills I had built in him. His success was visible; my role in creating that success was invisible.

Tyler now leads one of our most complex technical programs, using the stakeholder management framework I taught him. He handles difficult conversations with the collaborative approach I coached him through. He mentors his own team using the development architecture I designed. He solves problems by applying the systems thinking I spent years teaching him.

His excellence isn't evidence that he transcended what I taught—it's evidence that what I taught works at scale, in different contexts, with different personalities. This should feel like pure success. Instead, it required me to work through a difficult psychological transition.

For years, I'd operated under the assumption that there was a finite amount of recognition to go around. If Tyler became excellent at customer presentations by using my framework, somehow that diminished my expertise. If he created solutions by applying approaches I'd taught him, it made my contributions less visible. If he earned praise from senior management for executing my methods, it meant less praise would be available for me. That scarcity thinking was poisonous and completely wrong.

Tyler's success took nothing away from me. It multiplied what I could accomplish. When he handled customer relationships skillfully using techniques I'd developed, it freed me to focus on strategic challenges I'd never had time to address. When he mentored other team members with the framework I'd built, it created capability that extended far beyond what I could build personally. When he earned recognition, it reflected the effectiveness of the leadership development architecture I'd designed.

I redefined what technical leadership excellence looked like. Individual contributor excellence meant solving problems myself, demonstrating personal expertise, and being the go-to person for technical challenges. Technical leadership excellence meant creating frameworks that others could apply to solve problems I never could have tackled alone, developing systematic approaches that worked regardless of who executed them, and building teams that didn't need me to be the bottleneck for success.

The measure of a great technical leader extends beyond the problems they personally solve. Great leaders build systems that continue producing results when applied by others. Their frameworks prove robust enough to handle situations they never expected. When one person successfully applies their approach, it multiplies to enable three others to do the same, which then enables nine more.

Tyler's excellence was proof that I'd built something that worked: a teachable, repeatable framework for technical leadership that didn't depend on my personal presence to be effective.

More importantly, Tyler learned to apply this framework systematically. He used the structure I'd taught him to build psychological safety for his team. He implemented the stakeholder management techniques I'd shown. He coached others through the same development progressions I'd designed for him.

This was the multiplication effect I'd been trying to achieve. I was not just mentoring individuals, but creating systems that build leaders who can apply proven frameworks to create more leaders. That's a completely different game than individual technical achievement, and it's infinitely more rewarding once you learn to measure success by framework adoption rather than personal heroics.

The Accidental Mentoring Approach

On a particularly busy day, I had three different team members bring me similar problems. This was not where I needed to focus that day, but I needed my team to be successful, so I took the time to work with them. Each conversation took an hour. Each solution required my direct involvement. Each person walked away with a specific answer but no better ability to handle the next similar challenge. That evening, I calculated how much time I spent solving problems for others versus building their capacity to solve problems themselves. The ratio was embarrassing.

Through trial and error with Jordan, Tyler, Chris, and others, five principles emerged that consistently produced results:

- Start with their interests and motivation
- Focus on building thinking capability, not knowledge transfer
- Create learning sequences that build confidence
- Let people struggle with support available
- Coach the process, not the content

These weren't abstract theories. Each principle came from specific experiences where I succeeded or failed at developing someone's capability. Let me show you what each one looks like in practice.

Start with their interests and motivation.

My first attempt at systematic mentoring was a disaster. I identified three engineers I thought had "leadership potential" and created mentoring plans for each of them. I scheduled regular coaching sessions, designed stretch assignments, and prepared materials on technical leadership principles.

Two of the three went through the motions politely but showed no real engagement. The third stopped showing up for our coaching sessions after the first month. I solved the wrong problem. I was creating leaders based on my assessment of who should want to grow, rather than working with people who were actively seeking development.

Jordan taught me a better way. They approached me after a program review where I'd managed a tense conversation with a vendor who pushed back on our technical requirements. The vendor wanted changes that would compromise the design. I'd acknowledged their concerns, walked through our analysis, and found a path forward that addressed their business needs without sacrificing technical integrity.

After the meeting, Jordan came to my office. "I want to learn how to handle these kinds of conversations," they said. "I freeze up when people push back on my technical positions. I either get defensive, or I cave too easily. Would you be willing to help me develop these skills?"

Instead of my deciding what Jordan should learn, Jordan told me exactly what they wanted to develop. Instead of generic leadership development, we could focus on the specific capability they were motivated to build.

We started small. The next time a vendor meeting happened, I had Jordan prepare the technical position. We worked through how to expect pushback, how to acknowledge concerns without accepting conclusions, and how to build bridges while maintaining technical standards. I attended the meeting but let Jordan lead the conversation.

Jordan was nervous. They over-explained some points and missed opportunities to redirect unproductive discussions. The outcome was fine, but the execution was rougher than if I'd handled it myself.

Jordan came to my office afterward, feeling energized rather than deflated. "I see what you were doing now," they said. "Can we talk about what worked and what I should do differently next time?"

Over the following months, Jordan sought increasingly complex vendor interactions. They asked for coaching before difficult conversations. They reflected on what worked and what didn't. They developed their own approaches that built on what I'd taught them.

The difference between this experience and my failed first attempt was simple: Jordan wanted this growth. They were pulling themselves toward growth rather than having it pushed onto them. My role was to support what they were actively pursuing, not try to force them into something I thought they could be.

Now, at the beginning of any potential mentoring relationship, I ask explicitly: "What kind of growth are you interested in?" followed by, "How can I support your personal growth goals?" My job as a leader is to support their actual goals, not convert them to mine. When someone is genuinely motivated to develop a capability, mentoring becomes a collaboration. When they're not, it becomes an exhausting exercise in pushing against resistance.

Focus on building thinking capability, not knowledge transfer.

The shift from knowledge transfer to capability building is subtle but crucial. Early in my mentoring work, when someone asked, "How should I handle this stakeholder concern?" I would explain my approach, they'd execute my approach successfully, then come back with the next stakeholder question needing my guidance again. I created a dependency disguised as growth.

I learned to respond differently. When Tyler asked, "How do you decide when to push back versus when to accommodate?" I didn't give him my decision criteria. Instead, I asked, "What factors do you think matter in making that call?" His initial answer was incomplete, so I asked, "What else might be relevant?" Then, "How would you know if you were pushing back too hard?" Each question built his thinking framework rather than downloading mine.

Three weeks later, Tyler came to me with a different request. Instead of asking me what to do, he walked me through his thinking, "I'm seeing X concern from the customer, which suggests Y. I'm considering these three responses. Here's my assessment of the trade-offs." He thought independently, using frameworks he'd developed through our coaching conversations.

Teaching thinking capabilities takes longer than transferring knowledge, but it's the only approach that scales. When you give someone knowledge, they can handle situations that match what you taught them. When you build their thinking capability, they can handle situations neither of you expected.

Create learning sequences that build confidence.

My biggest mentoring mistake was throwing Chris, an aspiring technical leader, into a senior stakeholder presentation before he was ready. I recognized his potential and his desire for more visible responsibilities, so when a high-stakes opportunity came up, I assigned it to him. The presentation itself went reasonably well, but when stakeholders asked probing questions about budget and schedule implications, Chris struggled to respond confidently.

I'd made a classic error of confusing someone's technical competence with their readiness for political complexity. Chris had the knowledge but not the experience of reading stakeholder dynamics or managing conversations where multiple agendas were at play. I'd skipped the intermediate steps that would have built his confidence progressively.

After that experience, I redesigned Chris's mentoring path. Instead of jumping to senior stakeholder presentations, we created a sequence:

First, Chris presented technical reviews to our internal team. This was a supportive audience where mistakes had minimal consequences. This built his confidence in explaining complex concepts clearly.

Next, he presented to cross-functional teams within our program. These audiences asked challenging questions, but still within a collaborative environment. This taught him to expect different perspectives and adapt his communication.

Then he joined me in customer presentations, preparing the content while I handled the delivery. This let him see how I navigated stakeholder dynamics without the pressure of performing himself. Finally, he led customer presentations with me in the room as backup. By this point, he'd built the skills progressively rather than being thrown into complexity he wasn't equipped to handle.

I think of mentoring as a staircase, not an elevator. You can't skip steps and expect people to land on their feet. Each challenge needs to stretch someone just beyond their current capability while remaining within reach. Too easy, and there's no growth. Too hard, and confidence collapses under the weight of complexity they're not ready for.

The goal is designing progressions where each success builds the foundation for the next challenge, where people develop capabilities incrementally rather than being expected to make impossible leaps.

Let people struggle with support available.

Six months after I'd redesigned Chris' mentoring program, he was preparing for his first independent senior stakeholder presentation—one where I'd be in the room, but he'd be leading without my intervention. Three days before the meeting, Chris came to my office, visibly frustrated. He'd been working on the technical content for hours and couldn't figure out how to structure the presentation in a way that resonated with this audience.

My instincts urged me to take control. I saw exactly what the presentation needed. I could reorganize the content in twenty minutes and hand him a working structure. The meeting was important. The timeline was tight. Why let him struggle when I could just fix it?

Instead, I asked, "What's making this difficult?"

Chris felt he understood the technical details perfectly, but he couldn't figure out which aspects would matter most to stakeholders who cared more about budget and schedule than technical elegance. He'd tried three different approaches, and none of them felt right.

I resisted the urge to provide the answer. "Walk me through your three approaches. What was your thinking behind each one?"

As Chris explained his reasoning, I could see he was closer than he realized. He understood the stakeholder priorities—he just didn't trust his judgment enough to commit to a structure. He was struggling to build confidence in his thinking.

"Which approach do you think is strongest?" I asked.

Chris hesitated, then pointed to the second one. "This one feels most aligned with what they care about, but I'm worried it doesn't showcase enough of our technical depth."

"That's exactly the tension you need to manage in this presentation," I said. "You've identified the core challenge. Now, the question is, how do you show enough technical credibility without losing them in details they don't need?"

We spent the next thirty minutes with me asking questions, not providing answers. What signals would tell him he was losing the audience? How could he structure content to allow for different depths depending on the audience's interest? What would success look like from their perspective, not just ours?

Chris left my office with the same three approaches he'd brought in, but now he had a framework for deciding between them and the confidence to trust his own judgment. More importantly, he'd learned how to think through these trade-offs himself rather than depending on me to make the call.

The presentation went well, though not perfectly. Chris made a few choices I wouldn't have made. Some worked better than I expected. Some I would have handled differently. The presentation wasn't perfect, but Chris now had the thinking process to handle the next presentation with no need of me at all.

This was a different outcome than his first senior stakeholder presentation months earlier. That time, I'd thrown him in before he was ready, and he'd struggled. This time, after building his confidence through progressive challenges, he had the foundation to work through complexity with coaching support rather than needing me to solve it for him.

If I'd just given him the structure I knew would work, he would have delivered a better presentation that week. He also would have learned nothing about how to create structures for future presentations. I would have solved one problem while ensuring he'd need me to solve every similar problem going forward.

The most powerful learning happened when people worked through genuinely difficult challenges, knowing they could ask for guidance but weren't having problems solved for them. The struggle itself was the education.

Coach the process, not the content.

When preparing Tyler for his customer presentation, I could have told him exactly what to say. I could have scripted the opening, outlined the key points, and provided language for handling objections. He would have delivered my presentation successfully.

Instead, I coached him on how to prepare. We worked through the questions: How do you analyze what stakeholders care about? What signals tell you they're receptive versus resistant? How do you structure content for clarity versus completeness? How do you prepare for questions you can't anticipate?

The preparation took longer this way. In the end, Tyler was not only ready for this presentation; he was ready for any presentation. He'd learned a preparation process he could apply to different audiences, different technical content, and different organizational contexts.

This distinction between coaching content and coaching process shows up everywhere. When someone asks for help with a technical decision, I resist explaining what I would decide and instead explore how they might approach the decision-making. When someone struggles with a difficult conversation, I focus less on what they should say and more on how they can prepare for conversations with challenging dynamics.

The goal is to teach people how to fish, not to give them fish. Process knowledge transfers across situations. Content knowledge only works in the specific context where it was developed.

Developing and writing down these five principles gave me a fresh approach to leadership development. They weren't magic formulas. They were practices that required constant discipline to follow, especially when every instinct screamed at me to just solve the problem myself. The real test of these principles came when I realized that even successful mentoring can become unsustainable if it depends entirely on my individual capacity.

Reflection Framework: Assessing Your Mentoring Approach

Leadership Development Assessment: Are You Multiplying or Limiting Capability?

We all know how important mentoring is. In this reflection think when you're accidentally creating dependency instead of building leadership capability.

Are you mentoring people's capabilities or managing their work through them? There's a crucial difference between developing someone's judgment and having them execute your decisions with your oversight.

Do your team members become more confident and independent over time, or more dependent on your guidance? Real mentoring creates people who handle challenges you've never seen, people who handle challenges the way you would.

What makes you reluctant to delegate important work to others? Often our resistance can feel like it is about their capabilities, but it's really about our own need to be needed or fear of losing control.

What would happen to your team's capabilities if you were unavailable for six months? If the answer is "they'd struggle," you've been building dependencies rather than developing leaders.

One Thing to Try This Week

Identify one high-stakes opportunity that you could handle yourself but that would be a great development experience for someone on your team. Coach them through the preparation thoroughly but let them own the actual execution. Focus on what they'll learn from the experience rather than ensuring the outcome matches what you would have delivered.

Playbook:
Building Leaders Instead of Dependencies

When You Have a High-Stakes Opportunity

Sometimes, you have an important presentation or negotiation that you could handle yourself, but it would also be a great development opportunity for someone on your team.

Watch for when the stakes might be too high for development, people don't want the development opportunity, or you feel nervous about letting go.

Assess readiness honestly: "Do they have the technical foundation and communication skills to be successful with proper coaching?"

Provide thorough preparation: "What insights and strategies do they need to be effective in this situation?"

Stay available for support: "How can I be present to help without taking over?"

Focus on learning: "What will they gain from this experience that they can't get any other way?"

Letting go and allowing someone to step up is a big step for leaders who are used to handling difficult situations themselves. It's an important step to build up your team members to handle these situations on their own so you leave a legacy of competent leadership.

When Someone You're Mentoring Is Struggling

What do you do when someone you're trying to mentor is making mistakes and struggling with challenges that you could easily solve?

Watch for mistakes that are too costly for learning opportunities, people who need more foundational skills first, or your coaching approach not matching their learning style.

Resist the rescue urge: "What support do they need to work through this challenge themselves?"

Coach the thinking process: "Help me understand how you're approaching this problem."

Provide guidance, not solutions: "What options haven't you considered?" rather than "Here's what you should do."

Celebrate the learning: "What did you discover about your problem-solving approach through this experience?"

This scenario is where your discernment is important. You're trying to uncover whether this is a skill problem where you can support them or if this is a motivation problem and they're looking to offload responsibility. Pay attention to their behavior over their words. Actions speak much louder.

When You've Been Creating Dependencies

This one hits home. If you realize you've been solving problems for others rather than helping them grow their own problem-solving capabilities, try these ideas.

Watch for dependency patterns that are too entrenched, people who prefer the dependency, or your own need to feel important by being needed.

Change your response pattern: "What solutions have you considered?" before jumping in to help.

Create growth opportunities: "This would be great practice for your troubleshooting skills."

Set clear expectations: "I want to help you become more independent in handling these types of challenges."

Track progress: "How do you feel about your capability to handle similar problems in the future?"

This scenario speaks to leaders who easily step in when challenges arise and teams where they defer to a leader too quickly. In a fast-paced engineering world, it can feel like it would be faster to do it yourself, but in the long run, building a competent team speeds your production.

When Someone Avoids Disagreeing With You

When you find someone you're mentoring consistently agreeing with anything you say and avoiding any technical disagreement, the situation prevents real learning.

Watch for people who don't trust that disagreement is safe, previous experiences that taught them challenging authority is dangerous, or lack of confidence in their own technical judgment.

Create safe opportunities for disagreement: "I want you to challenge my thinking on this approach. What concerns do you have?"

Model vulnerability: "Here's where I'm uncertain about this decision. What's your take?"

Reward pushback: "I'm glad you're questioning this assumption. That's exactly the thinking we need."

Explain the learning value: "Disagreeing with me helps you develop your own technical judgment."

This seems counterintuitive. Leaders work to get consensus, so encouraging disagreement seems like the wrong path. While you don't want to encourage people to always push back, it's essential that your team feel safe to bring up disagreements so that when success is on the line, you don't miss key information.

When Fear of Mistakes Paralyzes Growth

Has someone you're trying to develop been paralyzed by the fear of making mistakes and won't take action without extensive checking with you?

Watch for perfectionism that's deeply rooted, anxiety from past failures, or fear that's rational given organizational consequences for mistakes.

Normalize imperfection: "Part of learning is making mistakes. I expect you to get some things wrong."

Create low-stakes practice opportunities: "This is a perfect situation to experiment because the consequences are manageable."

Share your own learning mistakes: "Here's how I messed up something similar early in my career and what I learned."

Focus on the decision-making process: "You're making good decisions with the information available. That's what matters."

Fear is a powerful motivator, and it keeps people stuck in what feels comfortable. You've been doing the work to grow your leadership capacity through the work in this book. Leverage that success with your team and give them the satisfaction of their own growth.

The Unsustainable Success

Becoming skilled at building technical leaders creates a whole new set of problems. The frameworks work. The mentoring multiplies. The organization gets stronger. Then you realize you've created something that depends on your continued involvement to keep growing. People want coaching on how to apply what you've taught them. They need guidance in situations you've navigated. They seek perspectives on the decisions they're facing.

You've solved the problem of being the person who has to do everything. Now you're becoming the person everyone needs to learn how to do everything well. It's progress, but it's not sustainable. I had built better systems for technical work, but I hadn't yet created sustainable systems for leadership development. I was still the bottleneck, albeit a fancier one.

I needed a system that helped me and the systems I was building develop leaders as a natural function, not as an additional burden on already-capable people. Going beyond looking for ways to increase efficiency, I needed to find a way to maintain this work over the long term without depleting myself in the process.

Moving to Systematic Architecture

The breakthrough came when I stopped thinking about mentoring as something I did for individuals and thought about it as emotional infrastructure I built for the organization.

Instead of carrying all the development conversations myself, I designed systems where peer mentoring happened naturally. Instead of being the only source of stretch opportunities, I created processes where challenging assignments were distributed based on development needs rather than immediate convenience. Instead of being the sole provider of feedback and coaching, I created cultures where multiple people could support each person's growth.

Sustaining Leadership
Without Losing Yourself

Chapter 9

I WAS EXHAUSTED. NOT the good kind of tired that comes from a challenging project well executed. The deep, bone-weary exhaustion that accumulates when you've been giving more than you have for too long.

After that successful test flight with Eric, Maria, Tom, and Sarah, I found myself in a new role as the vehicle lead—responsible for making sure all the details were in place to deliver the vehicle to our customer. Since then, I've been promoted to chief engineer, coached dozens of emerging leaders through the leadership development programs, and somehow become the person everyone turned to when human systems needed as much attention as technical systems.

I had become exactly the kind of technical leader I'd always wanted to be, but *I was burning out*. I'd spent years learning to read the room, to notice when team members were overwhelmed or struggling. I'd built frameworks for preventing upstream problems and building sustainable systems. I'd coached others on the importance of balance and self-care.

Unfortunately, I had failed to apply my own principles to the person who needed them most: me. By letting my own reserves hit zero, I'd corrupted the very emotional infrastructure I was trying to build. You can't draw a clean blueprint when your hands are shaking from exhaustion. In that state, I wasn't an architect; I was a firefighter who kept accidentally restarting the fire.

Sitting in my office late one evening, staring at yet another crisis that needed my attention, I realized I had a choice to make. I could continue being the heroic leader who solved every problem and mentored every person, gradually depleting myself until I had nothing left to give, or I could figure out how to sustain this work over the long term.

I needed to make this change for my wellbeing. I also needed to remember the example I was setting and the systems I was building.

Origin Story:
Hospitalization? Not me...

The hospitalization I mentioned in Chapter 7 was more than a wake-up call about an unsustainable pace. It was a complete system crash that forced me to confront the myths I'd been living by.

For years, I'd operated under the delusion that I could fuel myself with Advil and Diet Coke indefinitely. That willpower could overcome physiology. That taking care of everyone else's needs while ignoring my own was not only sustainable, but it was also somehow virtuous. I told myself that pushing through exhaustion was what good leaders did, that self-care was selfish when there was important work to be done.

During the recovery process, I was introduced to the "spoons" theory of personal capacity, originally envisioned by Christine Miserandino to explain life with chronic illness. The concept is elegantly simple: imagine you start each day with a finite number of spoons—let's say six. Every activity costs spoons. Some days, it costs three spoons to get out of bed and get the day started. On other days, maybe it's only half a spoon. Activities like chairing a failure review board might cost two or more spoons. A difficult stakeholder conversation could be a full spoon. An all-hands crisis response meeting might cost three.

Your capacity is finite. While you can spend more than your allocated spoons for the day, you're essentially borrowing them from tomorrow. Eventually, your spoon deficit will catch up with you. Sometimes that happens in dramatic ways, like ending up in a hospital bed wondering how you got there.

Learning to think in terms of daily energy allocation changed how I approached my work. Instead of saying yes to everything and then trying to find the energy somewhere, I asked, "What does this cost in terms of my finite daily capacity, and is that cost justified by the impact?" Some activities were energy-giving. Others were energy-draining. The goal was to balance the high-impact activities intentionally and to stop pretending that my capacity was unlimited.

My hospitalization taught me that sustainable leadership is about building systems that work because you're healthy enough to contribute to them long-term.

The Sustainability Paradox

The better you become at creating conditions for others to succeed, the more people want your help to create those conditions. Success creates a demand that can quickly become unsustainable.

I discovered this paradox after Tyler's successful customer presentation and the multiplication effect that followed. Word spread that I was good at mentoring emerging leaders. Suddenly,

I was getting requests from other programs to mentor their rising stars. Senior leadership asked me to coach struggling managers. People sought me out for advice on everything from technical decision-making to organizational dynamics.

What started as mentoring a few team members evolved into becoming the go-to person for leadership development across multiple organizations. I fielded requests to speak at conferences about technical leadership, to provide input on promotion decisions for people I'd never worked with directly, and to troubleshoot team dynamics for groups that weren't even in my organization. My success in building sustainable systems created an unsustainable demand for my time and energy. I became a choke point in the very systems I tried to optimize.

This isn't a problem you can engineer your way out of, which frustrated me. You can't schedule your way to sustainability, streamline your processes into balance, or analyze your way to having more energy. You must learn to be selective about where you invest your finite emotional and mental resources and accepting that saying no to good opportunities is often necessary to preserve capacity for great ones.

The Depletion Signals

The challenge with leadership burnout is that it doesn't announce itself with a dramatic moment of collapse. It creeps up gradually, masquerading as temporary stress or the normal demands of leadership responsibility. By the time you recognize what's happening, you're often already deep in the depletion cycle.

I noticed the warning signs during what should have been a routine week. Nothing was particularly wrong—no major crises, no impossible deadlines, no difficult stakeholder conflicts. Just the usual mix of technical decisions, mentoring conversations, and organizational coordination that I'd been handling successfully for months. Yet everything felt harder than it should have.

Decision fatigue was the first signal I recognized. I struggled to make simple choices that I'd normally make without thinking. Things like which meeting to attend when there was a scheduling conflict, how to prioritize competing requests for my time, even what to eat for lunch. I delayed decisions that should have been straightforward, creating a backlog of minor choices that accumulated into significant stress.

Emotional flattening followed close behind. The satisfaction that used to come from solving complex problems or watching someone have a breakthrough in their development was simply… gone. I went through the motions of the work I'd always loved. The emotional rewards that had sustained me through difficult periods had disappeared. Success felt mechanical rather than meaningful.

My curiosity—which had always been one of my strengths as a leader—diminished in ways that scared me. Instead of asking questions to understand the full context of a situation, I jumped to solutions based on pattern recognition. The patience for discovery, for sitting with ambiguity long enough to understand what was happening, was being replaced by an urgency to get to answers as quickly as possible.

Relationships that had been energizing felt transactional. The informal conversations—like coffee with emerging leaders, impromptu technical discussions, casual check-ins with team members—felt like additional drains on my capacity rather than sources of connection and insight. I avoided the very interactions that had originally drawn me to leadership work.

The physical symptoms were perhaps the most insidious because they developed so gradually that I adapted to each level of depletion until what once would have been unacceptable became my new normal. Sleep became elusive despite exhaustion. Tension settled in my shoulders and never fully released. Simple tasks that should have required minimal effort—like writing emails, preparing for routine meetings, even driving to work, felt like they were demanding more energy than I had available.

The dangerous part about these signals is that they normalize over time. What starts as "I'm having a tough week" becomes "This is what leadership feels like." You lose the reference point for what sustainable engagement feels like because depletion becomes your baseline.

Distributed Emotional Labor

I found myself in an unsustainable pattern I'd accidentally created. "Can you sit in on this vendor negotiation next Tuesday?" a program manager from a different organization asked. "You're so good at navigating these dynamics, and this vendor is being difficult about the technical requirements."

This was the third such request that week. People had noticed that I could read stakeholder dynamics and navigate difficult conversations effectively. Now I was being pulled into meetings across multiple programs, not because I had technical expertise in those systems, but because I could handle the human complexity. I'd become the emotional labor vending machine. Insert difficult conversation, get Lisa's intervention.

The immediate problem was time. I spent 15 to 20 hours per week in meetings where my primary contribution was managing interpersonal dynamics rather than technical content. Those hours were coming directly out of the time I needed for my actual responsibilities.

The deeper problem was what I was teaching. Every time I showed up to handle a difficult conversation with someone else,

I reinforced the belief that navigating stakeholder complexity required my personal involvement. I created sophisticated dependencies rather than building capability. I had a choice: I could keep saying yes and slowly drown in other people's emotional labor, or I could figure out how to help people handle these situations themselves.

The First Pushback

Angie, an engineer from another program, asked me to join a vendor negotiation that had become contentious. The vendor pushed back hard on our technical requirements, and Angie was convinced the meeting would go badly without my presence. My old pattern would have been to say yes, show up, navigate the dynamics successfully, and reinforce Angie's belief that she couldn't handle these situations without help.

Instead, I said, "Tell me about the meeting. What's making this difficult?" Angie looked surprised. "Well, the vendor keeps pushing back on our requirements. They say our specs are too rigid, and they want more flexibility. Every time we try to explain why the requirements matter, they get defensive." So, I asked, "What do they actually care about?" She then asked, "What do you mean?" I said, "The vendor. What's driving their pushback? What are they worried about?" Angie paused. "I... I'm not sure. I guess I assumed they were just being difficult."

We spent the next thirty minutes talking through what might motivate the vendor's resistance. Angie realized that what looked like an obstruction was probably the vendor trying to manage their own risk and cost constraints. Their pushback was quite rational from this perspective.

"Okay," Angie said, "I think I'm seeing this differently. But what if they bring up something I'm not prepared for? What if I handle it wrong and damage the relationship?"

"Then you'll learn something for next time," I said. "You know this system better than I do. You're not lacking technical knowledge—you're just nervous about the interpersonal complexity." "That's exactly what I'm nervous about," Angie admitted. "Which is why you need to practice," I said. "I'm here if you want to talk through your approach beforehand or debrief afterward. You need to build this capability yourself. Otherwise, you'll need me in every difficult stakeholder conversation for the rest of your career." Angie didn't love this answer, but she agreed to try.

The Messy Middle

The meeting didn't go perfectly. Angie told me afterward that she'd over-explained some technical points, gotten defensive when the vendor questioned our approach, and forgot to acknowledge their business constraints early in the conversation. "But," she said, sounding surprised, "we got to a workable solution. It wasn't as elegant as what you would have achieved, but we made progress." That's when I realized I was habitually asking myself the identical questions whenever I was summoned to a demanding meeting:

- What are the stakeholders actually worried about?
- What does success look like from their perspective?
- Where can we be flexible and where do we need to hold firm?
- How do we acknowledge their concerns without accepting their conclusions?

I wasn't doing anything magical in these meetings. I was just asking those questions systematically before walking into the room. If I could get people to think through those questions themselves, they wouldn't need me there. Over the next several months, I repeated this pattern. When someone asked me to attend their difficult meeting, I'd spend 30-45 minutes asking them questions about the stakeholders, the dynamics, and what they were trying to achieve. Then I'd send them in without me.

The resistance was significant and consistent. People wanted a quick fix of having me present rather than the messier process of figuring it out themselves. Program managers worried that letting people learn through imperfect execution would jeopardize important relationships. Some meetings went badly. People made mistakes I could have prevented. A few relationships got temporarily strained. I had to resist the urge to jump back in and "just handle it" when things got rough.

I also had to get comfortable with the fact that people weren't executing these conversations the way I would have. They had different styles, different approaches, and different strengths. That was okay—good, even. The goal was to help people develop their own capabilities for navigating complexity.

The Gradual Shift

I worked on this for a long time. The dynamic shifted gradually. Angie sought me out before difficult conversations to talk through her approach, not to ask me to attend. Other engineers noticed and did the same. People asked each other the same questions I'd been asking them. Someone created a shared document where people captured what worked and what didn't in difficult stakeholder conversations—not as a formal process, just as informal notes. Others added to it. People referenced it when preparing for their own challenging meetings.

My meeting requests for "Can you sit in on this difficult conversation?" dropped from 15 to 20 hours per week to maybe 5 hours per month—and those were typically situations that genuinely needed my specific technical expertise or organizational authority, not just general stakeholder management capability.

More importantly, people were getting better at this work. They were developing their own pattern recognition about stakeholder dynamics, their own confidence in managing difficult conversations, their own judgment about when to be flexible and when to hold firm.

The Unexpected Cost

The discomfort of this transition surprised me, even though it was evidently working. When I wasn't in these meetings, I couldn't control the outcomes. People made choices I wouldn't have made. Some relationships took longer to repair than if I'd handled things myself. A few opportunities were lost because someone wasn't as skilled at reading the room as I was.

I had to get comfortable with good enough rather than perfect. The organization gained distributed capability at the cost of some short-term optimization. That trade-off felt wrong to my engineering brain, which wanted to maximize every outcome. I also had to confront how much of my identity had been wrapped up in being the person who could handle difficult conversations. When I stopped being needed for that, I felt… less valuable. Less central. Less indispensable. That was the point, of course. Knowing something intellectually and being comfortable with it emotionally are different things.

The Real Architecture

Looking back, the system I'd built grew past stakeholder navigation techniques or meeting preparation. It was about changing the default assumption from *difficult conversations require Lisa* to *difficult conversations require preparation and practice*. Instead of one person who could navigate complexity well, we developed multiple people who could handle these situations competently. Not perfectly, not the way I would have done it, but well enough to keep making progress. This new architecture created an environment where people were expected and supported to develop these capabilities themselves rather than depending on someone else to handle the hard parts for them.

When I wasn't constantly depleted from carrying everyone's emotional labor, I had significantly more capacity for the strategic challenges that genuinely required my involvement. When I participated in stakeholder conversations, I could focus on complex organizational dynamics rather than basic meeting management. When I coached people, I was more patient because I wasn't resentful about the time it took. This was what sustainable leadership looked like—not heroic individual performance, but capability that continued growing even when I wasn't personally present.

How This Shows Up Everywhere: The Finite Capacity Reality

The pattern started in college, though I didn't recognize it as a pattern until much later.

Every semester, I'd push through increasingly demanding coursework, managing heavy technical loads and maintaining what I thought was a reasonable social life. I'd tell myself I needed to make it to finals, then to the end of the semester, then I could finally relax and enjoy all the things I'd been putting off.

Without fail, within forty-eight hours of my last final exam, I'd come down with a cold or flu that would sideline me for most of my break. The very vacation time I'd been looking forward to—the chance to sleep in, see friends, maybe read something that wasn't a textbook—would be spent in bed, sick and frustrated that my body had betrayed me at exactly the wrong moment.

I chalked it up to bad timing. Stress was suppressing my immune system. The bad luck of being around sick people during the exam period. It never occurred to me that this was my body's way of demanding the rest and recovery I'd been denying it for months.

I didn't recognize this as a warning about finite capacity because I was operating under the myth that mental and emotional energy worked differently than physical energy. I understood you couldn't run a marathon every day without consequences, but I somehow believed that emotional and intellectual intensity could be sustained indefinitely through willpower and caffeine.

The semester crash pattern was my first introduction to what I now understand as the spoons theory, though I wouldn't have the language for it until much later.

The same pattern followed me into my professional life, showing up after every major project delivery. I'd push through complicated program milestones, working long hours and managing multiple crises, fueled by adrenaline and the promise of things calming down once we hit the next major milestone. Then, as soon as the pressure let up, my system would crash. What should have been celebration time became recovery time.

It happened after the wedding I'd planned meticulously, vacations that required extensive coordination, and major program deliveries where I'd been operating in crisis mode for weeks. I could push myself through to the end. Once that external pressure disappeared, my system would come crashing down, seeking the rest and recovery I'd been denying it. Even positive events like hosting family gatherings, organizing team celebrations, and taking on exciting stretch assignments would leave me depleted afterward in ways that seemed disproportionate to the actual work involved.

I learned that emotional and mental energy have limits as real as physical energy. You can borrow against tomorrow's capacity, but eventually, the bill comes due. Sometimes you don't have a choice about spending more than you have. Crisis situations, family emergencies, and critical project deadlines require you to dig deep and find reserves you didn't know existed.

It became clear that planning for the subsequent recovery time was essential. A self-aware leader recognizes when they've been operating in overdraft mode and builds in deliberate rest before they're forced to take it. I was intentional about this pattern instead of being surprised by it. I'd add an extra day between travel and needing to be at work, so I wasn't showing up sleep-deprived and irritable. I became very deliberate about accepting meetings immediately after completing major projects, knowing I'd need time to process and recharge. I learned to see recovery time not as weakness or poor planning, but as a necessary part of sustainable high performance.

The finite capacity reality applies to everything: decision-making energy, emotional availability for difficult conversations, patience for mentoring others, creativity for solving complex problems. Once I thought in terms of energy allocation rather than time management, I could be much more strategic about when and how I engaged with high-cost activities.

Setting Boundaries When Everyone Expects Availability

The email situation had been building for months before I recognized it as a problem. I'd check my phone before getting out of bed in the morning. During breakfast. In the car at stoplights. Between meetings. During dinner. Before bed. Sometimes at 2 AM when I woke up and couldn't get back to sleep. I told myself I was just staying on top of things. Being responsive. Making sure nothing fell through the cracks. The truth was, I'd trained myself—and everyone around me—to expect constant availability.

One Friday evening, when I was having dinner with my family, my phone buzzed with an email from a program manager asking about a technical review scheduled for the following Tuesday. Not urgent. Not time-sensitive. Just a routine question that could easily wait until Monday morning. I picked up my phone to respond. My youngest looked at me and said, "You're always on your phone."

Ouch. That stung.

I put the phone down, but the email nagged at me through the rest of dinner. What if the program manager was waiting for my response to move forward with something? What if my delay caused problems? What if people thought I was becoming less committed to the work?

After dinner, I responded to that email and three others that arrived during the meal. Then I checked to see if there were any new ones. It then dawned on me that this situation was unworkable and, more significantly, unproductive. I was constantly interrupted, rarely fully present anywhere, and modeling exactly the burnout behavior I'd been coaching others to avoid.

The Decision

On Monday morning, I stopped checking email outside of work hours. No complex rules about what counted as urgent. No exceptions for important projects. Just work hours only. I added a line to my email signature: "I send and read emails during business hours. If you need immediate help outside those hours, please call." It felt simultaneously reasonable and terrifying.

The reasonable part: of course, people shouldn't expect instant email responses at 9 PM or 6 AM. That's not how urgent communication should work, anyway.

The terrifying part: what if people thought I didn't care anymore? What if I missed something critical? What if this damaged my reputation as a responsive leader?

I didn't announce the change in a team meeting or send out a policy memo. I just stopped. Stopped checking email after 7 PM. Stopped checking it before 7 AM. Stopped checking it on weekends unless I was explicitly on call for a critical issue.

The Immediate Pushback

The first week was…*interesting*. Tuesday evening at 8:30 PM, a program manager emailed asking for input on a presentation he was giving to senior management the next morning. I saw the notification on my phone. I didn't respond.

Wednesday morning, I arrived at work to find a follow-up email sent at 6:45 AM. "I guess you didn't see my message in time. I had to make my best guess about the approach. Would have been helpful to have your input." The implied criticism was clear: I'd let him down by not being available. I replied, "I saw your email this morning. For future reference, if something needs my input before the next business day, please call me so I know it's time-sensitive. My email turnaround is next-business-day for everything that isn't urgent enough to require a phone call." His response came within minutes. "Got it. I didn't realize you weren't monitoring email anymore." That *anymore* felt loaded; like I'd changed the rules of some agreement we'd all made about constant availability.

The Pattern Continues

Over the next few weeks, similar situations played out repeatedly. A colleague emailed at 10 PM and made a comment the next morning about how "some of us work late to get things done." The implication being that my 9 AM response time showed less dedication.

A senior manager mentioned in a meeting that I used to be more responsive. "I remember when you'd get back to people right away, even in the evenings. Have you taken on too much?" Someone scheduled a meeting during a block of time I'd marked as unavailable and then expressed frustration when I declined, saying, "I thought you were committed to this effort." Each instance required me to hold the boundary again; to explain that immediate email response outside business hours wasn't beneficial to anyone. I shared that if something genuinely needed urgent attention, there were better ways to communicate it than email. I reminded the team that being responsive during business hours was sufficient for nearly everything we worked on. Some people accepted this easily. Others kept testing the boundary, as if my resolve might weaken if they pushed hard enough.

The Internal Struggle

The external pushback was uncomfortable but manageable. My internal struggle was worse. Every evening when I didn't check email, part of me worried I was missing something important. Every morning when I opened my inbox to find 15-20 messages that had arrived overnight, I felt behind before the day even started. When someone made a comment about my reduced availability, I questioned whether I was being selfish. Was this boundary necessary, or was I just being less committed to the work?

The temptation just to *check quickly* was constant. It would take thirty seconds to scan my inbox and make sure nothing was on fire. What was the harm in that? The harm, I had to keep reminding myself, was that *just checking quickly* never stayed quick. One check became five. One response led to three more emails. The boundary dissolved the moment I made an exception.

The Shift

The change happened gradually, but the emails never stopped. My inbox was still a 24/7 repository for every thought, update, and "just checking in" note the organization could produce. The real shift was in the categorization of urgency.

Because I had been consistent with the "call me if it's urgent" rule, people had to perform a mental calculation before reaching out. They had to ask themselves: "Is this worth a phone call at 8 PM?" For 99% of the issues that previously would have had me hunched over my laptop during dinner, the answer was a resounding no.

The emails still arrived, but the invisible tether of expectation had been cut. My colleagues stopped expecting an immediate reply to a late-night message because they'd learned I wouldn't even see it until morning. Instead, the boundary acted as a filter. If something was truly on fire, my phone rang. And interestingly, it rang far less than I feared it would. When the phone did ring, I answered it without resentment because I knew it was legitimate. For everything else, I had regained my evenings.

When I wasn't constantly interrupted, when I had an actual separation between work and personal time, I came to work less depleted. I was more patient in coaching conversations. I was more creative in problem-solving because my brain had been "offline" for twelve hours. I was more able to focus during critical technical discussions because I wasn't already exhausted by a three-hour "email war" that started before breakfast.

A few people even thanked me for the boundary, saying it gave them permission to set similar limits themselves. "If Lisa isn't available 24/7, maybe I don't need to be." One engineer told me, "I used to think being a leader meant always being on. Watching you set boundaries without apologizing for them made me realize that's not true." We weren't just changing a communication habit; we were reclaiming the headspace required for actual engineering.

The Unexpected Lesson

It was not the boundary's functionality that proved most astonishing. It was in how much resistance revealed about organizational dysfunction. The people who pushed back hardest on my boundary were often the ones whose own work-life balance was most unsustainable. My boundary forced them to confront their own patterns of constant availability, and they didn't appreciate the mirror.

The senior managers who questioned my commitment were often the ones modeling the crisis-hero leadership I'd spent years trying to prevent. My boundary challenged the implicit norm that dedication was measured by availability rather than effectiveness.

By establishing boundaries, I not only safeguarded my energy but also revealed the organization's reliance on unsustainable habits that had become standard practice. There was an expectation of continual availability simply because it had always been provided, resulting in a downward spiral where maintaining limits seemed like betraying the team.

My boundary didn't just change my own patterns. It changed expectations more broadly. Not universally, not quickly, but gradually. Other people set similar limits. Managers questioned whether the late-night email culture was beneficial or just performative.

The Ongoing Work

Even now, the boundary requires maintenance. New people join the organization and assume I'm available 24/7 because that's how they're used to working. Projects hit critical phases where the pressure to be constantly available intensifies. My instinct to "just check quickly" never completely goes away.

The boundary isn't a onetime decision. It's a practice that requires constant reinforcement, especially when external pressure makes it feel easier to just give in. What makes it sustainable is that I'm no longer alone in holding it. Enough people have adopted similar boundaries that it's becoming more normal to have limits rather than exceptions. The organizational culture is shifting slowly from expecting constant availability to respecting designated work hours. That cultural shift didn't happen because I announced a policy or made an interesting argument for work-life balance. It happened because I held a boundary consistently enough that other people felt safe doing the same.

Recognizing and Recovering from Depletion

It was during a seemingly ordinary meeting with a junior engineer that I understood I was utterly drained. Marcus had asked for the meeting to talk through a technical decision he was struggling with. I usually enjoy this kind of conversation—helping someone work through their thinking, asking questions that open up new perspectives, watching them have breakthrough moments.

Instead, I barely listened. While Marcus explained the technical trade-offs he was weighing, I was mentally drafting an email to a different program, worrying about a stakeholder meeting scheduled for later that afternoon, and thinking about the three other items on my to-do list that I should have already finished.

Marcus asked me a question. I had to ask him to repeat it because I genuinely hadn't heard what he said. "Sorry," I said, "could you say that again?" He repeated the question. I gave him an answer that was technically correct but completely unhelpful—the generic advice that didn't engage with the specific complexity he was facing.

Marcus looked disappointed but thanked me for my time anyway. After he left, I sat there realizing I'd just delivered the worst mentoring conversation I'd had in years. I realized I had nothing left to give. I was running on empty, and it was corrupting everything I touched.

Taking Stock

That evening, I honestly assessed my capacity using the spoons framework. On a good day, I had about six to eight spoons to work with. Some days more, some days less, but this was a reasonable baseline. I listed out what I'd been doing regularly:

- Leading technical reviews: 2 spoons
- Mentoring conversations: 1-2 spoons each (and I was doing 3-4 per week)
- Crisis management: 2-3 spoons per incident (happening 2-3 times per week)
- Stakeholder relationship management: 1-2 spoons per difficult conversation (daily)
- My actual chief engineer responsibilities: 2-3 spoons per day
- Preparation for all the above: another 1-2 spoons

I was spending 10-12 spoons daily when I only had six. I'd been doing this for three months straight, ever since we'd hit a critical program milestone that never quite stopped being critical. The math was brutal and undeniable. I was systematically depleting myself, borrowing from tomorrow's capacity to handle today's demands, and accumulating a deficit that was now affecting my ability to do anything well. My hospitalization years earlier should have taught me this lesson. Apparently, I am a slow learner.

The Recovery Plan

I didn't have the luxury of taking a month off to recover. Our program was in a critical phase. People were depending on me and I had responsibilities that couldn't just be paused while I recharged. What I could do was stop spending 10-12 spoons daily and get back to something closer to 6. That meant being ruthless about what required my personal involvement versus what I'd taken on because I could do it well or because people expected me to handle it.

I made a list of everything I was currently doing and sorted it into three categories:

- Only I can do this: chief engineer technical decisions, certain stakeholder relationships where my organizational authority mattered, specific mentoring commitments I'd already made.
- Someone else should do this: Most of the crisis management (we had capable engineers who could handle these with coaching), many of the stakeholder conversations (people needed to build this capability themselves), some of the technical reviews (I didn't need to attend every one personally).
- Nobody needs to be doing this right now: several "improvement initiatives" I'd volunteered for that weren't urgent, documentation projects that could wait, conference presentations I'd agreed to that were still months away.

Just looking at the list was exhausting. I'd taken on so much that even delegating it felt overwhelming.

The Delegation Conversation

On Monday morning, I had a really difficult conversation with my manager. "I need to offload about 30% of what I'm currently doing," I told him. "I'm depleted to the point where I'm not doing anything well." I expected pushback. We were in a critical program phase. This was the worst possible time to reduce my workload. Instead, he asked, "What took you so long to say something?"

His question surprised me. I said, "I thought I could manage it. I kept thinking that if I just got through this next milestone, things would calm down." He replied, "They never calm down. You know that. What do you need?"

We spent the next hour going through my list. Some things he could reassign directly. Others required negotiation with other program leads. A few initiatives just stopped, at least temporarily.

The hardest part was my mentoring commitments. I'd promised to coach several people and reducing that felt like letting them down. We worked out a compromise where I'd continue with my current mentees but wouldn't take on any new ones for at least three months. Some of my current mentees would transition to peer coaching arrangements with other experienced leaders.

The Guilt Phase

For the first two weeks after delegating work, I felt terrible about it. I watched people struggle with problems I could have solved quickly. A technical decision took three days longer than it would have if I'd just handled it myself. A stakeholder conversation went poorly because the person leading it wasn't as experienced as I was at reading the room.

Every imperfect outcome felt like evidence that I'd been wrong to step back; that I was being selfish; that my need for recovery was coming at the cost of program success. I had to keep reminding myself that what I was seeing was the short-term cost of building long-term capability. These people needed to develop these skills. They wouldn't develop them if I kept swooping in to handle everything.

The guilt was especially intense around the mentoring relationships I'd stepped back from. One engineer I'd been coaching sent me a question via email. I directed him to another senior leader who could help. He responded with a short "ok thanks" that felt distinctly cool. I wanted to apologize, to explain, to make sure he understood it wasn't personal. Instead, I had to accept that sometimes protecting your capacity means disappointing people, and that's okay even when it's uncomfortable.

The Slow Recovery

Recovery didn't happen on a predictable timeline. After two weeks of reduced load, I expected to feel better. I didn't. I was less exhausted, but the decision fatigue, emotional flattening, and reduced curiosity were still there. Apparently, you can't undo three months of depletion in two weeks.

After a month, I noticed small improvements. I had energy for conversations at the end of the day instead of just counting down the minutes until I could leave. I had ideas again instead of just reacting to whatever was in front of me. I could focus on one task at a time instead of constantly mentally multitasking.

It took about six weeks before I felt like I was functioning at my normal capacity instead of less depleted than before. Even then, I could feel how fragile that recovery was. One week of returning to old patterns and I could slide right back into depletion.

What Actually Helped

My recovery went far beyond reducing workload, although that was necessary. I needed to rebuild the practices I'd abandoned during the crisis period. I slept seven hours again instead of six (or five, or four). That alone probably made more difference than anything else, though it felt impossibly indulgent at first. I stopped working through lunch. I took a break, went outside, and talked to people about non-work topics or read a book. Thirty minutes of genuine disconnection in the middle of the day turned out to be worth far more than the thirty minutes of "productivity" I'd been squeezing in. I reinstated my morning routine that I'd been skipping in favor of getting to work earlier. Twenty minutes of coffee and reading something not work-related before diving into email made an enormous difference in my mental state for the entire day.

These weren't radical self-care practices. They were basic maintenance that I'd convinced myself I didn't have time for. Turns out, not having time for basic maintenance is how you end up completely depleted.

The Support System

What made my recovery sustainable was having people who could see my patterns more clearly than I could. My manager checked in weekly: "How are you doing, really?" Sometimes I'd insist I was fine when I clearly wasn't, and he'd point to specific evidence I was taking on too much again.

A colleague I trusted agreed to be my *boundary accountability partner*. When I was tempted to take on something new, I'd run it by her first. She got fantastic at asking, "Do you actually have capacity for that, or are you saying yes because it's interesting?"

My family called me out when I checked email at dinner or worked evenings when I'd said I wouldn't. That external accountability was essential because my judgment about my capacity was clearly not reliable.

The Planned Relapse: The Artemis II Mission

There is a difference between a boundary that collapses and a boundary that is intentionally lowered for a specific, high-stakes reason. I learned this distinction during the Artemis II mission.

For months, I lived in a state of suspended animation. I was on standby, waiting for the vehicle to be ready for launch. Because I knew I would be in Houston for at least two, and possibly three weeks once the clock started, I couldn't schedule anything that couldn't be easily shifted or canceled. I was planning for the support I'd need around my house while I was gone, clearing my desk of work products that required deep focus, and avoiding critical meetings that I might have to walk out of mid-sentence.

When we finally got the green light and I booked my flight, the shift was immediate and total. For twelve days, it was a full-on press. We worked around the clock, fueled by the heavy responsibility of ensuring the mission's success and, more importantly, the crew's safety.

In many ways, it looked like a total relapse into the behaviors that had put me in the hospital years before. I didn't sleep enough. I didn't get in my regular gym time. I didn't keep up with my routine work. I barely had time to talk with my family. But there was one fundamental difference: this time, I was the one in control of the trade-off.

I knew this surge was a possibility, so I treated it like a marathon rather than a frantic scramble. Even in the middle of the non-stop effort, I worked hard to eat well. I made it to the gym—not as often as I'd like, but enough to stay grounded. I didn't have hour-long calls with my family, but I made it a point to connect over text throughout the day to stay tethered to my life outside the mission.

The most important part of the strategy, however, was the plan for what happened after. In the past, I would have returned from a mission like that and immediately tried to "catch up" on everything I'd missed, driving myself back into the ground. This time, I committed to taking time off the moment I returned home. I am now being as intentional about my "slow re-entry" as I was about the mission itself.

I've learned that technical leadership sometimes requires a 100% effort that is simply unsustainable long-term. The key is recognizing when you are in a "sprint" season and having the discipline to return to your boundaries as soon as the mission is accomplished. A relapse is only dangerous when it becomes the new permanent state. When it's a conscious choice with a planned recovery, it's just part of the job.

What I Learned

Depletion isn't a onetime event you recover from and then never face again. It's a pattern you must manage actively throughout your career. The warning signs—decision fatigue, emotional flattening, reduced curiosity, treating interactions as transactional—those don't go away. They're always lurking, ready to show up whenever you push too hard for too long. The difference lies in how fast you spot them and how ready you are to act before they totally ruin your performance.

I learned that I'm terrible at assessing my capacity. I need external accountability from people who can see my patterns more clearly than I can. I need systems that force me to pause and honestly evaluate whether I'm spending more spoons than I have.

I learned that recovering from depletion requires accepting temporary inefficiency. Things will take longer. Some outcomes won't be as perfect as they would have been if I'd handled them myself. People will be disappointed that I'm not as available as I used to be.

That's the cost of sustainable leadership. The alternative of burning myself out completely doesn't serve anyone in the long run, no matter how productive it feels in the short term.

Reflection Framework: Assessing Your Sustainability

Sustainability Audit: Can You Maintain This Pace?

Sustainable leadership is about building systems that let you maintain effectiveness over years and decades rather than burning out after intense periods.

Examine Your Current Patterns

Where are you borrowing energy from tomorrow to handle today's demands? Notice when you're consistently staying late, skipping meals, or cutting into recovery time to manage your workload.

What early warning signals are you experiencing that might indicate depletion? Decision fatigue, emotional flattening, reduced curiosity, or treating routine interactions as drains rather than connections.

How do others respond when you try to set boundaries around your availability? If people expect you to be constantly available or always say yes to requests, your boundaries aren't boundaries.

What would happen to your team's effectiveness if you were unavailable for a month? If they'd struggle without your constant involvement, you haven't built sustainable leadership structures.

One Thing to Try This Week

Block two hours on your calendar for strategic thinking. This time cannot be used for crisis management or meeting attendance. It needs to be actual planning and reflection time. Protect this time as fiercely as you'd protect a critical technical review. Notice how difficult it is to maintain this boundary and what that tells you about your current sustainability patterns.

Playbook:
Recognizing and Addressing
Unsustainable Patterns

When You Face High-Pressure Periods

Try these ideas when you're entering a critical project phase where the temptation to abandon sustainable practices feels overwhelming.

Watch for rationalizing unsustainable practices as temporary, pressure too intense for any boundary-setting, or believing you're different from everyone else who's burned out this way.

Recognize the pattern: "High-pressure periods make boundaries more critical, not less important."

Set minimum standards: "What are the absolute minimum recovery practices I need to maintain effectiveness?"

Plan for recovery: "I'll block time for restoration immediately after this intensive period ends."

Use external accountability: "I'll check in with someone who can help me see my patterns clearly."

Having a system in place for when you know life will be busy or there's a lot of pressure to deliver will keep you from falling back on habits. Know your self-care non-negotiables and make sure you set clear timelines for when you'll get back to your normal routines.

When People Push Back on Your Boundaries

Try these when colleagues or stakeholders resist your efforts to set healthy limits around your availability.

Watch for when you're taking others' resistance personally, have boundaries that conflict with genuine organizational needs, or are inconsistent in maintaining limits when pressure increases.

Explain the benefit: "These boundaries enable me to be more effective when I am available."

Stay consistent: "My boundaries aren't negotiable, *and I'm committed to finding ways to meet your needs within them*."

Recognize the pattern: "Pushback often comes from people whose own unsustainable practices my boundaries are exposing."

Don't absorb their anxiety: "Their discomfort with my boundaries is information about organizational dysfunction, not evidence I should abandon them."

People who get upset at your boundaries are the reason you need boundaries. Especially as you establish your time and energy as a priority, people who benefitted from your over-performance get upset. Be strong, restate your boundary, and keep going. You've got this.

When You're Already Experiencing Burnout

As you review your week, you notice you're showing signs of depletion and need to rebuild capacity while maintaining performance.

Watch out for trying to fix everything at once, minimizing the seriousness of depletion, or believing you can willpower your way through systematic exhaustion.

Acknowledge the reality: "I've pushed beyond sustainable limits and need to address this systematically."

Prioritize ruthlessly: "What are the absolute essential activities that only I can do right now?"

Get an external perspective: "I need someone who can help me see patterns I'm too depleted to recognize myself."

Accept temporary inefficiency: "Recovery takes time and energy that feels like it could be spent on 'productive' work."

Burnout is easy to slip into and difficult to get out of. Building up a support system in advance can prevent you from getting stuck in unsustainable situations. Know your essential needs and prioritize meeting them. Acknowledge that you can't be everything to everyone, so be the best of who you can be and ask for help from others to fill in the gaps.

When Success Creates Unsustainable Demand

It can feel great to see leadership success until your effectiveness at building leaders and solving problems creates more requests than you can handle.

Watch out for being flattered by requests that are dumping in disguise, identity too tied to being needed, or organizations that don't support distributed leadership development.

Recognize the sustainability paradox: "My success at developing others has created a new type of dependency."

Distinguish between urgent and important: "Not every request that feels urgent requires my immediate personal attention."

Build capability in others: "How can I help people develop independence rather than creating more sophisticated dependency?"

Set meta-boundaries: "I need limits not just around individual requests, but around the total volume of development work I take on."

Successful leadership demands that you create a sustainable pace and assign to others the tasks that you don't need to tend to personally. It is easy to want to answer all the questions from people who aspire to learn from you. This is why I wrote this book—so I can point my readers here instead of sharing the same stories on repeat.

The Foundation for What Comes Next

You can't be an effective emotional architect while running on empty. You can't build others' capabilities while depleting your own. The frameworks in this book work only when applied consistently, especially under pressure.

Every skill we've explored—reading rooms, building trust, navigating conflict, making sustainable compromises, preventing crises, developing leaders—requires emotional and mental resources to execute well. When you're depleted, you default to old patterns: becoming defensive instead of curious, solving problems instead of building capability, rushing toward crises instead of preventing them.

The depletion signals I learned to recognize were indicators that my leadership effectiveness was compromised. I knew I was in trouble when decision fatigue hit. Sometimes, I stared at a lunch menu for ten minutes, paralyzed by the choice between a turkey sandwich and a salad because my brain simply had no more deciding left in it.

Most critically, exhaustion corrupted my ability to architect sustainable systems. When I was depleted, I reverted to the same crisis heroics and emotional labor absorption that I'd spent years learning to prevent. Instead of designing systems where others could handle challenges independently, I jumped back into rescue mode because it felt faster than coaching others through their growth.

I was inadvertently creating the very dependencies I'd been trying to eliminate. My burnout was systematically undoing the emotional infrastructure I'd built.

I realized sustainable leadership is about modeling what's possible for the people I'm mentoring. When emerging leaders see you burning yourself out to achieve results, they learn that effectiveness requires self-destruction. When they see you maintaining boundaries while delivering excellence, they learn that sustainability and high performance enable each other.

Your approach to sustainability becomes part of the organizational culture. When you design systems that enable your own long-term effectiveness, you're simultaneously teaching others how to build systems that enable theirs. When you demonstrate that excellent results don't require heroic self-sacrifice, you're creating cultural infrastructure that makes sustainable excellence possible for everyone.

The leaders you mentor will carry forward your technical frameworks and, more importantly, your approach to sustainable leadership. If you include dysfunction in your own work patterns, you're teaching them to include dysfunction in theirs. The real measure of our work is whether these skills create self-sustaining, ever-improving systems after we're gone.

The Ultimate Architectural Challenge

Often, leaders are assessed on their ability to assess situations, foster trust, manage disagreements, or cultivate leaders. For me, the measure of my knowledge is whether I can design systems that continue creating technical excellence and human flourishing long after I was no longer there to maintain them personally.

This meant designing emotional infrastructure that was self-sustaining rather than dependent on my individual capacity. It meant creating cultures where psychological safety, collaborative problem-solving, and leadership development happened naturally rather than requiring constant intervention.

The most successful leadership work is invisible. It is so embedded in how people work together that it feels like 'that's how we do things here' rather than something that requires maintenance and oversight.

In our final chapter, we'll explore how to build legacy systems that outlast your direct involvement. Organizations that continue creating technical excellence and human flourishing long after you've moved on to new challenges.

Building Legacy Systems

Conclusion

FIVE YEARS AFTER that perfect flight test, I found myself back at Kennedy Space Center for a program review. Walking through the same high bay where Eric, Maria, Tom, and Sarah had once been labeled as "difficult," I watched a new team working with the same focused collaboration that had made our original mission successful.

The team leader facilitating the technical discussion wasn't someone I'd trained directly. The quality engineer who caught potential issues early wasn't someone I'd mentored personally. The way they navigated disagreement—using curiosity instead of defensiveness, asking questions that revealed underlying concerns—wasn't something I'd taught them.

Eric noticed me watching from the observation deck and joined me. "Pretty amazing, isn't it?" he said. "That team leader learned those facilitation techniques from Maria. The quality engineer is using the upstream thinking approach Tom developed. None of them has ever worked directly with you."

That's when I understood what legacy systems look like. I admired how the people I influenced were influencing others, creating unforeseen and uncontrollable ripple effects, rather than by the frameworks I'd documented or the processes I'd designed.

This is the ultimate test of technical leadership: what continues to work after you're no longer there to maintain it personally.

How Emotional Architecture Propagates

The people you develop become carriers of better leadership practices throughout their careers. Maria now mentors quality inspectors on multiple spacecraft programs, teaching them not just what to look for but how to raise concerns in ways that strengthen relationships. Eric leads cross-functional teams using room-reading skills to spot when technical discussions are being derailed by unspoken concerns. Tom has become an early warning system across multiple programs, teaching others to think upstream. Sarah mentors emerging leaders in productive disagreement.

None of them replicates what I did. They've adapted the principles to their contexts, their personalities, their challenges. They've made the team dynamics better. More importantly, they're teaching others. The engineers Tyler mentored early in his career are now program managers at different companies, spreading these approaches across the aerospace industry. A quality engineer who learned upstream thinking from Maria is teaching those approaches at her new company, preventing crises in programs I'll never hear about.

This is how emotional architecture scales: individual → team → organization → industry. Each person who learns to build trust quickly, prevent problems systematically, and mentor others rather than hoard knowledge changes every organization they touch. Your influence extends far beyond your direct reports, your current program, and your organization's walls.

The true measure of success goes beyond the achievements of the current team to the lasting impact of the leaders you cultivate and how they contribute to the performance of every team they join throughout their professional journeys.

The Architecture That Sustains Itself

True legacy systems have specific characteristics that distinguish them from temporary improvements imposed by individual leaders:

The practice becomes invisible. When systems work so well that people forget they needed to be learned, you've succeeded. New team members quickly adapt to the culture of curiosity over defensiveness, upstream thinking over crisis response, development over dependency because "that's how we do things here." The psychological safety feels natural, not manufactured.

The system improves itself. People empowered to think rather than just execute continue finding better ways to handle complexity. Each challenge becomes an opportunity to refine approaches rather than abandon them.

Multiple people can teach the principles. Emotional architecture isn't dependent on charismatic individuals. The frameworks work regardless of who's applying them, transferring across different communication styles and leadership approaches.

The culture survives leadership transitions. It's embedded in everyday practices rather than dependent on inspirational messaging or personal relationships. The most successful leadership culture is so deeply embedded that it feels like "just how we work" rather than something requiring constant maintenance.

The View from Kennedy Space Center

A few months ago, I stood near the launchpad at Kennedy Space Center, looking at the hardware that will soon carry the Artemis II crew toward the Moon.

It is easy to look at that stack and see only the metal, the tiles, and the fuel. When I look at it, I see a map of thousands of hard conversations. I see the moments where an engineer had the courage to say, "I don't know" in a room full of experts. I remember design reviews where someone shared a half-baked idea that ended up solving a critical failure mode. Behind every weld and sensor is an emotional architecture that held together under the weight of immense pressure.

My role as Chief Engineer eventually shifted, as all roles do. The systems I helped architect—the way the team communicates, the way they share risk, and the way they protect one another's psychological safety—remain.

That is the goal of this book. Whether you are building a mobile app, a medical device, or a lunar spacecraft, your job is to build a system that can eventually outgrow you. Artemis II isn't just a mission to the Moon; it's a testament to what happens when we stop trying to be the exhausted hero and start being the architect of something that lasts.

When those engines ignite, they are fueled by every honest conversation, every shared risk, and every piece of emotional labor that went into making that moment possible. We don't go to the Moon just because we have the best rockets; we go because we've built the human systems capable of carrying us there.

Your Work Begins Now

You now have the foundation for building legacy systems in your organization:

- You can read both technical and human systems simultaneously, spotting when human dynamics block technical progress.
- You can build trust that enables difficult conversations.
- You can navigate conflict in ways that strengthen relationships.
- You can make decisions that balance technical ideals with practical constraints.
- You can think upstream to prevent problems rather than heroically solve them.
- You can develop leaders who multiply your impact.
- You can sustain this work without depleting yourself.

You understand that technical excellence and human flourishing aren't competing priorities—they enable each other.

These aren't separate leadership skills. They're integrated components of emotional architecture. Trust-building makes conflict navigation possible. Upstream thinking prevents crises that destroy psychological safety. Leadership development multiplies capacity across your entire organization.

You won't do this perfectly. You'll misread rooms. You'll damage trust and will need to repair it. You'll make compromises that feel uncomfortable. You'll miss problems you should have caught upstream. You'll struggle with letting go as you develop others. You'll need to protect your own capacity when every instinct tells you to push harder.

The difference is that you now have frameworks for recognizing these patterns and correcting course. You understand that leadership effectiveness comes from systematic approaches, not individual heroics.

Start with your next difficult conversation. Notice what the room needs that isn't being said. Build trust through small moments of consistency. Navigate the conflict toward understanding rather than victory. Ask yourself what problem you're preventing six months from now. Consider who else could handle this with proper coaching. Check whether you can engage fully. Then build from there.

Create conditions where your team members feel safe surfacing problems, challenging ideas, admitting uncertainty. Design systems that catch issues early rather than managing them heroically. Develop people who can think independently rather than depending on your expertise. Model sustainability so others learn excellent results don't require self-destruction.

Your legacy will be the people you mentored who solve problems you never could have tackled alone. The systems you build that continue improving after you're gone. The culture you build that makes both technical excellence and human flourishing feel natural rather than forced.

The future needs more technical leaders who understand that the hardest problems aren't technical at all. They're human problems showing up in technical clothes. Go build something that changes how people experience technical work. Build something that outlasts you. Build something that makes the impossible feel inevitable.

The teams you build, the leaders you develop, the problems you prevent, and the capabilities you create will ripple forward in ways you'll never fully see. That's the nature of legacy systems. They work best when they've become so embedded that no one remembers they needed to be built.

A Personal Note

This book grew out of my journey of learning to lead humans as skillfully as I design systems. Every framework, every story, every insight emerged from real situations where I had to figure out how to navigate the intersection of technical excellence and human complexity.

The work isn't finished. It never is.

I want to be honest about what this transformation required because the leadership books that make it sound easy do a disservice to anyone attempting real change.

Learning to read rooms meant accepting how much I'd missed before. It was seeing how many times I'd steamrolled over concerns I didn't see, dismissed perspectives I didn't understand, or created solutions that solved technical problems while creating human ones. The awareness was often painful before it became useful.

Building trust as an outsider meant accepting vulnerability, which I'd spent years avoiding. It meant admitting mistakes publicly, acknowledging limitations openly, and depending on others in ways that felt terrifying for someone who'd built their identity on technical competence and self-reliance.

Navigating disagreement without defensiveness required confronting my own ego in ways that were deeply uncomfortable. I had to learn the difference between being right and being effective, between winning arguments and solving problems. Some of my most important leadership growth came from moments when I was completely wrong about something I was certain I understood.

Learning to make sustainable compromises meant accepting that "perfect" solutions that kill programs aren't perfect. It meant getting comfortable with decisions that made the engineer in me cringe, but served the mission. It meant learning to hold complexity without rushing to simplistic answers.

The hardest lesson was learning to build others' capabilities, even when it meant they might eventually surpass my own. Watching Tyler handle that customer presentation better than I could have was simultaneously the most threatening and the most satisfying moment of my leadership career.

You can't build healthy emotional systems for others while carrying your own unexamined dysfunction. The personal healing was foundational to this work. Every unresolved pattern in your own emotional landscape becomes a blind spot in the systems you design for others. Every place where you lack self-awareness becomes a place where your architecture fails. The journey to becoming an Emotional Architect requires building your own emotional infrastructure first.

What I Didn't Expect

Technical leadership has been both harder and more rewarding than I expected when I started this journey. It requires more emotional intelligence and less individual heroics than I thought. It demands more patience and offers more satisfaction than I had imagined.

I didn't expect how much leadership would change my relationship with technical work itself. Understanding human systems made me a better systems engineer. Learning to build trust made me more effective at technical collaboration. Developing others' capabilities multiplied what we could accomplish together in ways I never could have achieved alone.

I didn't expect how much personal healing this work would require, or how it would transform every relationship in my life. You can't build psychological safety for others while carrying your own unexamined wounds. You can't help others navigate conflict if you're avoiding your own difficult conversations. The frameworks for reading rooms, building trust, and navigating disagreement changed not just my technical leadership but my relationships with my children, my friendships, my capacity for handling life's inevitable conflicts and changes.

Most of all, I didn't expect how much more fulfilling it would be to enable others' success than to achieve my own.

What I Want You to Know

If you're reading this book because technical leadership feels overwhelming, you're not alone. The transition from individual contributor to leader of people is one of the most challenging career transformations you'll ever attempt. It requires developing entirely new skills while maintaining excellence in your technical domain.

If you're struggling with the human complexity that surrounds technical work, that struggle is normal and necessary. The discomfort you feel when stakeholders seem irrational, when team members resist good ideas, when politics interferes with sound engineering, is information. It's telling you that the technical solution alone isn't sufficient.

If you feel like you're failing at leadership while succeeding at technical work, you're probably in the middle of the most important learning of your career. The gap between individual excellence and leadership effectiveness is where all the real growth happens.

If you're exhausted from being the person who must solve every problem, carry every relationship, and manage every crisis, this book is your permission to build something more sustainable. You don't have to be the hero. You can be the architect.

The Continuing Journey

Writing this book has reminded me why this work matters so deeply. Every time someone chooses curiosity over defensiveness, every time a team feels safe enough to surface problems early, every time a leader develops someone else's potential, we're proving technical excellence and human dignity aren't competing values.

The ripple effects of emotional architecture extend far beyond any single organization or project. The leaders you build will carry these approaches into new roles, new companies, and new challenges we can't yet imagine. Each conversation you navigate skillfully, each crisis you help prevent, each person you mentor becomes part of a larger movement toward technical organizations where both excellence and humanity thrive.

The frameworks you've learned are more than professional tools. They are a way of seeing that will change how you show up in every relationship and challenge. Once you understand emotional architecture, you can't unsee the human systems operating in every context. You'll find yourself designing better family dynamics, designing more effective friendships, and building emotional infrastructure that serves every community you're part of. Your leadership skills will determine how far you can go from here.

The future needs technical leaders who can hold both the rigor of engineering and the messiness of humanity. Leaders who can solve complex problems while building the people capable of solving even more complex problems. Leaders who can be simultaneously technically excellent and emotionally intelligent.

That future is waiting for what you'll create—not alone, but together with the people you'll develop, the trust you'll build, and the systems you'll design to outlast your own involvement.

Build well. Lead sustainably. Enable awesome.

Acknowledgments

The people who shaped this book extend far beyond those named in the dedication, and I am grateful for the community that made this work possible.

To the team members whose stories form the backbone of these pages — while names and details have been changed to protect privacy, your experiences and your growth taught me everything I know about emotional architecture. Your willingness to trust, to question, to fail, and to try again created the laboratory where these insights emerged.

To my colleagues in aerospace leadership, who provided the complex, high-stakes environment where emotional intelligence stops being a concept and becomes a survival skill. Working alongside engineers, technicians, and program managers who care deeply about both technical excellence and human connection has been the privilege of my career.

To the countless leaders, managers, and individual contributors who have shared their challenges, frustrations, and breakthroughs with me over the years — every conversation about difficult stakeholders, impossible deadlines, and team dynamics that refuse to make sense contributed to this book's understanding of how the human variable shapes technical outcomes.

To the researchers and authors whose work gave language to what I was living long before I had words for it. Standing on your shoulders made it possible to see further.

To my publisher and the team who believed this book needed to exist, and then did the work to bring it into the world.

To every technical leader who has ever felt exhausted by the human complexity of their role — while still caring too much to walk away. This book exists because you deserve support for the hardest parts of the job that no one talks about. You are exactly who I wrote it for.

About the Author

Lisa Akers has spent 35 years doing what most technical leaders are never trained to do: engineering the human side of high-stakes work with the same rigor applied to rockets.

As Chief Engineer for NASA's Orion human spaceflight program at Lockheed Martin—including the Artemis II mission designed to carry humans around the Moon—Lisa has spent nearly two decades

at the intersection of technical excellence and human complexity. A Silver Snoopy Award winner, she is one of aerospace's most trusted voices on what it actually takes to lead people who do dangerous, consequential work.

Her path was anything but linear. She majored in English before finding her way to aerospace, served in the Air Force in space operations, led cross-functional launch teams, stepped away for five years to raise her children, and returned to the space world with a sharper eye for the patterns that make or break technical organizations. That combination of literary training, military discipline, and decades of high-stakes leadership shaped the Emotional Architect framework—a systematic methodology for building the human systems that determine whether technical systems succeed or fail.

Lisa founded the Human Variable Institute to formalize what she learned the hard way: that emotional labor is a systems problem, not a personality problem; that "difficult" people are usually the product of dysfunctional environments; and that sustainable technical excellence requires leaders who can read human context as fluently as they read data.

She is a sought-after speaker, mentor to emerging technical leaders across the aerospace industry, and a passionate advocate for normalizing the specific challenges that high-performing women face—at work, in relationships, and in the quiet space between ambition and exhaustion. She is the mother of two remarkable young men who have taught her more about leadership than any program ever could.

The Emotional Architect is her first book.

Visit her at LisaAkers.com, connect with her on LinkedIn, or invite her to speak at your next event.

About the Publisher

ArmLin House is an independent publisher and production company specializing in books and media that educate, entertain, and elevate their creators. We work with authors, entrepreneurs, and professionals to develop powerful stories—from memoirs and business books to instructional and illustrated works—and guide them from idea to finished product.

Our process blends coaching, editorial development, design, and production, ensuring each project is professionally formatted and ready for release in print, digital, audio, or video formats. Whether authors choose to publish independently or through ArmLin House, we provide the tools, structure, and expertise needed to bring their work to market with clarity and confidence.

Beyond publication, we help creators position and promote their work through strategic written and visual assets designed to reach a worldwide audience. At ArmLin House, we don't just produce books—we help creators turn their knowledge, experience, and stories into lasting, impactful media.

More Info
armlinhouse.com